HEAVY BAG
WORKOUT

A HARD-CORE GUIDE TO HEAVY BAG WORKOUT ROUTINES

BOOK 3 OF A CONTINUING SERIES

SAMMY FRANCO

Also by Sammy Franco

Heavy Bag Combinations
Heavy Bag Training: For Boxing, Mixed Martial Arts & Self-Defense
The Complete Body Opponent Bag Book
Invincible: Mental Toughness Techniques for Peak Performance
Unleash Hell: A Step-by-Step Guide to Devastating Widow Maker Combinations
Feral Fighting: Advanced Widow Maker Fighting Techniques
The Widow Maker Program: Extreme Self-Defense for Deadly Force Situations
Stand and Deliver: A Street Warrior's Guide to Tactical Combat Stances
Maximum Damage: Hidden Secrets Behind Brutal Fighting Combinations
First Strike: End a Fight in Ten Seconds or Less!
The Bigger They Are, The Harder They Fall
Self-Defense Tips and Tricks
Kubotan Power: Quick & Simple Steps to Mastering the Kubotan Keychain
Gun Safety: For Home Defense and Concealed Carry
Out of the Cage: A Guide to Beating a Mixed Martial Artist on the Street
Warrior Wisdom: Inspiring Ideas from the World's Greatest Warriors
Savage Street Fighting: Tactical Savagery as a Last Resort
War Machine: How to Transform Yourself Into a Vicious and Deadly Street Fighter
1001 Street Fighting Secrets
When Seconds Count: Self-Defense for the Real World
Killer Instinct: Unarmed Combat for Street Survival
Street Lethal: Unarmed Urban Combat

Heavy Bag Workout: A Hard-Core Guide to Heavy Bag Workout Routines (Book 3 of a Continuing Series)
Copyright © 2015 by Sammy Franco
ISBN: 978-1-941845-17-2
Printed in the United States of America

Published by Contemporary Fighting Arts, LLC.
Visit us Online at: **SammyFranco.com**
Follow us on Twitter: **@RealSammyFranco**

For author interviews or publicity information, please send inquiries in care of the publisher.

Caution!

The author, publisher, and distributors of this book disclaim any liability from loss, injury, or damage, personal or otherwise, resulting from the information and procedures in this book. This book is for academic study only.

The information contained in this book is not designed to diagnose, treat, or manage any physical health conditions.

Before you begin any exercise or activity, including those suggested in this book, it is important to check with your physician to see if you have any condition that might be aggravated by strenuous training.

About this book

Heavy Bag Workout is my third book in the Heavy Bag Training Series. This comprehensive book features over two dozen "out of the box" workout routines that will maximize your fighting skills for boxing, mixed martial arts, kickboxing, self-defense, and personal fitness.

With over 100 detailed photographs and step-by-step instructions, Heavy Bag Workout has beginner, intermediate and advanced workout routines that will make you hit faster and harder than ever before!

This unique book provides step-by-step instructions for performing a wide range of beginner, intermediate and advanced heavy bag workout routines. Whether you're an elite fighter or a complete beginner, this comprehensive book will take your fighting skills to the next level and beyond!

The exercises featured in this book are based on my 30+ years of research, training and teaching the martial arts and combat sciences. I have taught these unique drills to thousands of my students, and I'm confident they will help you reach higher levels of performance.

This book assumes you currently possess the basic punching skills. However, for those of you who need a quick refresher course, I have provided step-by-step instructions for all of the punching techniques in the appendix of this book. In addition, you will also find a glossary of terms. Since this is both a skill-building workbook and training guide, feel free to write in the margins, underline passages, and dog-ear the pages.

Finally, I encourage you to read this book from beginning to end, chapter by chapter. Only after you have read the entire book should you treat it as a reference and skip around, reading those topics that directly apply to you.

Train hard!

- Sammy Franco

VIII

PRELIMINARY STUFF

Heavy Bag Refresher

Before we begin with the workout routines, it's important to go over a few important things. For some of you this information will be enlightening, for others it will serve as a good refresher. Regardless of your training experience, these fundamental concepts are timeless and will benefit anyone.

Benefits of Heavy Bag Training

As I discussed in *Volume 1* of this book series, *Heavy Bag Training: For Boxing, Mixed Martial Arts, and Self-Defense*, the heavy bag is a fantastic piece of training equipment that provides a full range of benefits for the practitioner. Some of these benefits include:

- Developing and sharpening your fighting skills.
- Conditioning your entire body for the rigors of intense fighting.
- Improving muscular endurance.
- Strengthening your bones, tendons, and ligaments.
- Conditioning your cardiovascular system.
- Relieving stress and channeling aggressive energy in a productive manner.
- Developing several mental toughness attributes, such as instrumental aggression, immediate resilience, self-confidence, and attention control.

Finding the Right Heavy Bag

The heavy bag is constructed of either top grain leather, canvas or vinyl. Most bags are 14 inches in diameter and 42 inches in length. The interior of the bag is filled with either cotton fiber, thick foam, sand or other durable material. Depending on the brand, heavy bags can weigh anywhere from seventy-five to two hundred and fifty pounds.

The Heavier, The Better!

The weight of the heavy bag is probably the most important consideration when making a purchase. As a rule of thumb, try to buy the heaviest bag you can afford. Remember, when it comes to heavy bag training, *the heavier, the better!* If possible, avoid buying a bag that weighs under 100 pounds. Anything lighter won't provide sufficient resistance against powerful punches. As a result, the bag will swing uncontrollably when working out. I use a 150-pound heavy bag in my training. It offers the ideal amount of resistance for intense power punching sessions.

When looking to buy a heavy bag, avoid purchasing it from your local sporting goods store, as most of these bags are cheap, poorly made, and won't provide years of reliable use. The heavy bag is a serious piece of training equipment, so you should spare no expense and look for the highest quality brand that you can afford.

The good news is you can find a reasonably priced quality bag on the Internet. Here are just a few reputable companies that stand by their products:

- Ringside Equipment (ringside.com)
- Combat Sports, Inc (combatsports.com)
- Title Boxing (titleboxing.com)
- Everlast Equipment (everlast.com)

If possible, avoid purchasing a self-standing punching bag. While these "fitness bags" might look like a heavy bag, I can assure you they are not. In fact, these bags are poorly designed and cannot withstand the striking power of a heavy hitter.

The Best Places to Workout

Safe and effective heavy bag training will require you to find a place that will allow both you and the bag to move around freely. The location should also be a relatively quiet place that is free of distractions. Here are a few places you might want to consider:

- Garage
- Carport
- Basement
- Barn
- Home gym (if you are fortunate enough)
- Open field or backyard
- Warehouse
- Under a deck

Heavy Bag Gear

Before you begin working out, invest in a good pair of bag gloves that will protect your hands. When buying gloves, spare no expense and look for a high-quality brand. This will provide years of reliable use and will help ensure a better quality workout.

Bag gloves are constructed of either top grain cowhide or durable vinyl. There are two styles of bag gloves sold on the market:

- *Mitt style gloves*
- *Finger style gloves*

If you don't think you'll need bag gloves, think again. Striking the heavy bag without hand protection causes sore knuckles, bruised bones, hand inflammation, sore wrists, and scraped knuckles. These minor injuries will set your training back for several weeks in order for your hands to heal. However, for those of you who are interested in bare-knuckle training, I discuss it in the next chapter.

Boxing Gloves

Boxing gloves can also be used for heavy bag training. In fact, boxing gloves are often used by advanced practitioners for developing arm strength and endurance.

The ideal boxing glove is one that provides comfort, protection, and durability. Depending on your training objective, the glove can weigh anywhere from ten to sixteen ounces.

Here are some important features to be aware of when purchasing a pair of boxing gloves:

- To avoid wrist injuries, the glove should fit snugly.
- The boxing glove should be composed of multi-layered foam padding.
- The glove should have a sufficient palm grip that provides comfort and fist stabilization.
- To avoid a thumb injury, the glove should have thumb-lock stitching.
- The glove should be double-stitched to ensure durability.
- The entire glove should be constructed of top-quality materials to increase its durability.

Heavy Bag Workout

- The glove should be relatively easy to slip-on and off your hands. Velcro fasteners are sometimes preferred over laces.

Hand Wraps

Hand Wraps (also called wrist wraps) are used by experienced athletes who want an added measure of protection to their hands and wrists when hitting the heavy bag. They provide support to the entire hand and wrist area and can help prevent osteoarthritis in later years.

Essentially, hand wraps are long strips of cloth measuring two inches wide and nine to eighteen feet long. The longer hand wraps are more often used by practitioners who have large hands and who wish to have greater hand protection. You can find hand wraps at most sporting goods stores as well as the Internet.

Hand wraps should only be used in conjunction with either large bag gloves or boxing gloves. Do not strike the heavy bag with just your hand wraps as this can easily injure your hands.

Hand wraps are washable and should be cleaned after every workout. Although there are many hand wrapping techniques, the procedures shown on page 7 is suggested.

While hand wraps are a necessary piece of training equipment for boxing and other combat sports, I don't recommend using them for self-defense training. Reality based self-defense training requires you to condition your hands to withstand bare-fisted striking.

Boxing gloves can also be used if your knuckles are too sore or bruised to hit the heavy bag. The extra padding can make all the difference between skipping a workout and sticking with your routine.

How to Apply Hand Wraps

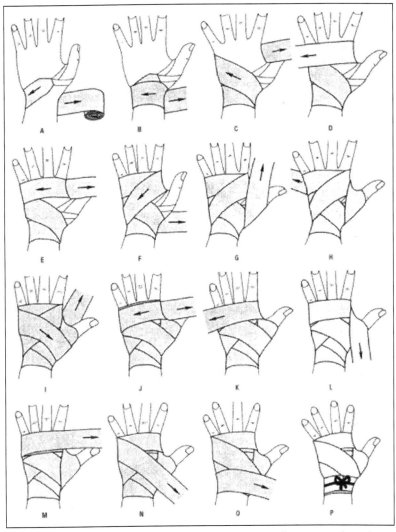

How to wrap your hands and wrists with hand wraps. Follow steps A through P.

Interval Workout Timer

Since heavy bag training is structured around time and rounds, you should invest in a good workout timer. Boxers, mixed martial artists, and kickboxers will use workout timers to keep track of their time during their rounds.

Most workout timers will allow you to adjust your round lengths anywhere from 30 seconds to 9 minutes. Rest time can be set from 30 seconds to 5 minutes depending on your level of conditioning and training goals.

There are several professional timers sold on the market, and they vary in price. Be forewarned! Some of them can be very pricey. However, there are numerous smartphone apps that replicate the same function and characteristics of an actual interval timer. These workout timer apps are convenient and very inexpensive. Your best bet is to search the Internet or your favorite app store for one that meets your specific needs.

Workout Timers are great for:

- Keeping track of the number of rounds and the time of each round.
- Measuring your current level of cardiovascular conditioning.
- Monitoring your progress in your heavy bag training.
- Creating healthy competition in your heavy bag routine.

Important Training Tips

Here are some important tips when working out on the bag:
1. Always warm up with some light stretching and calisthenics before working out.
2. Gradually build up the force of your blows. Remember, a beginner's wrists are too weak to accommodate full-force punches.

3. Never sacrifice your balance for power.
4. Remember to snap your punches.
5. Always keep your wrists straight when striking the bag.
6. Always maintain proper form.
7. Move around and avoid remaining stationary.
8. Learn to blend your strikes into logical combinations.
9. Pace yourself to avoid premature exhaustion.
10. Don't wear jewelry or a watch when training.
11. Stay relaxed and avoid unnecessary muscular tension.
12. Never hold your breath. Remember to exhale with the delivery of each and every technique.
13. Avoid the urge to stop the bag from moving. Let it swing freely!
14. If you don't know the proper way to throw a punch or kick, get instruction from a qualified coach or instructor.
15. Avoid heavy bag training two days in a row. Give your body a few days to recover from your last workout.

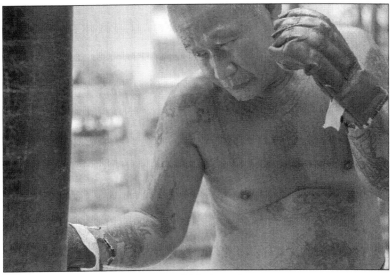

You are never too old for heavy bag training.

Get a Check-Up First

Heavy Bag training is extremely intense and very taxing on your heart. So, before you begin any exercise program, including those suggested in this book, it is important to check with your doctor to see if you have any condition that might be aggravated by this type of strenuous exercise.

Warming Up

Before beginning any of the drills, it's important that you first warm up and stretch out. Warming up slowly increases the internal temperature of your body while stretching improves your workout performance, keeps you flexible, and helps reduce the possibility of an injury.

Some of the best exercises for warming up are jumping jacks, rope skipping or a short jog before training. Another effective method of warming up your muscles is to perform light and easy movements with the weights.

When stretching out, keep in mind that all movements should be performed in a slow and controlled manner. Try to hold your stretch for a minimum of sixty seconds and avoid all bouncing movements. You should feel mild tension on the muscle that is being stretched. Remember to stay relaxed and focus on what you are doing. Here are seven stretches to get you started.

- **Neck stretch** - from a comfortable standing position, slowly tilt your head to the right side of your neck, holding it for a count of twenty. Then tilt your head to the left side for approximately twenty seconds. Stretch each side of the neck at least three times.

- **Triceps stretch** - from a standing position, keep your knees slightly bent, extend your right arm overhead, hold the elbow of your right arm with your left hand, and slowly pull your right elbow to the left. Keep your hips straight as you stretch your triceps gently for thirty seconds. Repeat this stretch for the other arm.

- **Hamstring stretch** - from a seated position on the floor, extend your right leg in front of you with your toe pointing to the ceiling. Place the sole of your left foot in the inside of your extended leg. Gently lean forward at the hips and stretch out the hamstrings of your right leg. Hold this position for a minimum of sixty seconds. Switch legs and repeat the stretch.

- **Spinal twist** - from a seated position on the floor, extend your right leg in front of you. Raise your left leg and place it on the outside of your right leg. Place your right elbow on the outside of your left thigh. Stabilize your stretch with your elbow and twist your upper body and head to your left side. Breathe naturally and hold this stretch for a minimum of thirty seconds. Switch legs and repeat this stretch for the other side.

- **Quad stretch** - assume a sitting position on the floor with

You need a good stretching program designed to loosen up every muscle group. Remember, you can't kick or punch, or otherwise execute the necessary body mechanics if you're "tight" or inflexible. Stretching on a regular basis will also increase the muscles' range of motion, improve circulation, reduce the possibility of injury, and relieve daily stress.

your hamstrings folded and resting on top of your calves. Your toes should be pointed behind you, and your instep should be flush with the ground. Sit comfortably into the stretch and hold for a minimum of sixty seconds.

- **Prone stretch** - lay on the ground with your back to the floor. Exhale as you straighten your arms and legs. Your fingers and toes should be stretching in opposite directions. Hold this stretch for thirty seconds.
- **Groin stretch** - sit on the ground with the soles of your feet touching each other. Grab hold of your feet and slowly pull yourself forward until mild tension is felt in your groin region. Hold this position for a minimum of sixty seconds.

Avoiding Overtraining & Burnout

Burnout is defined as a negative emotional state acquired by physical overtraining. Some symptoms of burnout include physical illness, boredom, anxiety, disinterest in training, and general sluggish behavior. Whether you are a beginner or expert, you're susceptible to burnout. Here are a few suggestions to help avoid burnout in your training:

1. Make your workouts intense but enjoyable.
2. Vary your training routine (i.e., hard day/easy day routine).
3. Train to different types of music.
4. Pace yourself during your workouts - don't try to do it all in one day.
5. Listen to your body- if you don't feel up to training, skip a day. Missing a day or two won't kill you.
6. Work out in different types of environments.
7. Use different types of training equipment.
8. Work out with different training partners.

9.   Keep accurate records of your training routine.

10. Vary the intensity of your training throughout your workout.

What's Next?

Now that we covered the preliminary stuff, it's time to move on to the actual heavy bag routines. So, if you're ready, let's move on to the next chapter.

Heavy Bag Workout

THE WORKOUT ROUTINES

The Three Training Methodologies

Before introducing you to the heavy bag routines featured in this chapter, it's important to first discuss the three training methodologies.

Essentially, all of the heavy bag routines presented in this book will fall under one of three different types of training methods; they are proficiency training, conditioning training, and street training. Let's take a look at each one.

Conditioning Training

Conditioning Training focuses exclusively on "time-based" workouts and it's primarily used by boxers, mixed martial artists, kickboxers, self-defense technicians, and fitness enthusiasts who wish to train on the heavy bag for specified period of time called *rounds*. Depending on the practitioner's level of conditioning, each round can range anywhere from one to five minutes. Each round is then separated by either 30-second, one-minute or two-minute breaks. A good heavy bag workout consists of at least five to eight rounds.

Conditioning Training is performed at a moderate pace, and it develops cardiovascular fitness, muscular endurance, fluidity, rhythm,

Conditioning training can also be used when sparring, shadow boxing, skipping rope, and focus mitt training.

distancing, timing, speed, footwork, and balance. Many fitness enthusiasts who are looking to burn fat will use this methodology as it tends to burn a significant amount of calories.

Conditioning Training does require that you have a fundamental understanding of combining punches and kicks together into logical combinations.

As I discussed in *Volume 2* of this book series (*Heavy Bag Combinations: The Ultimate Guide to Heavy Bag Punching Combinations*), a combination or *compound attack* is the logical sequence of two or more techniques thrown in strategic succession. For example, a jab followed by a rear cross is considered to be a basic punching combination.

Proficiency Training

The second training methodology is Proficiency Training and it's generally used by martial artists and self-defense practitioners who want to sharpen one specific punch, kick, or strike at a time by executing it over and over for a prescribed number of repetitions. Each time the technique is performed with "clean" form at various speeds. Punches are also carried out with the eyes closed to develop a kinesthetic "feel" for the action.

Proficiency Training on the heavy bag develops speed, power, accuracy, non-telegraphic movement, balance, and psychomotor skill.

Proficiency training is not just limited to martial arts and self-defense. It can also been used by boxers who want to develop and sharpen a specific punching technique. For example, a boxing coach might have his student jab at the bag for a specific amount of repetitions.

Street Training

The third and final training methodology is Street Training, and it's specially designed for reality-based self-defense preparation.

Since most self-defense altercations are explosive, lasting an average of 20 seconds, the practitioner must prepare for this possible scenario. This means delivering explosive and powerful compound attacks with vicious intent for approximately 20 seconds, resting one minute, and then repeating the process. Well-conditioned athletes can go longer. In fact, a few of my students are capable of performing the street training methodology uninterrupted for a full minute.

Street Training prepares you for the stress and immediate fatigue of a real fight. It also develops speed, power, explosiveness, target selection and recognition, timing, footwork, pacing, and breath control. You can also practice this methodology in different lighting, on different terrains, and in various environmental settings.

Street Training is not just limited to heavy bag training. For example, you can prepare yourself for multiple assailants by having your training partners attack you with focus mitts from a variety of angles, ranges, and target postures. For 20 seconds, go after them with vicious and powerful offensive techniques.

Street training is predicated on explosiveness. The offensive techniques that barrage the bag should possess a sudden and immediate outburst of violent energy. Your attack should never be progressive in nature; it does not build in speed and power. It begins and ends explosively.

Technique Always Comes First!

Take your time when working out on the heavy bag. If you are learning how to use it for the very first time, I strongly urge you to take your time and develop the proper punching mechanics before tearing into the bag.

Remember, the heavy bag is a serious piece of training equipment, and it is easy to get injured when using it. Heavy bag workouts are also tough and very demanding on the body. Avoid premature exhaustion by pacing yourself during your workouts. Remember, it's not a race! Enjoy the process of learning how to use the bag with skill and finesse.

Again, before you begin any of the exercise programs included in this book, it's important to check with your doctor to see if you have any condition that might be aggravated by strenuous exercise.

Finally, it's time to take a look at the different types of heavy bag workouts. I'll start with the conventional methods first and then work our way to the most obscure methods of heavy bag training.

Workout Routine #1
Time-Based Training

A time-based heavy bag workout is based on rounds, and it's an ideal way to structure your workouts. Before you begin, decide on the duration of your rounds as well as the rest intervals.

In most cases, mixed martial artists, boxers and kick boxers will work the heavy bag for three-minute rounds with one-minute rest periods. Depending on their level of conditioning and specific training goals, they might do this for a total of 5 to 10 rounds.

Initially, you'll need to experiment with both the round duration and rest intervals to see what works best for you. Remember to start off slow and progressively build up the intensity and length of your workouts. Don't forget to work with the bag and not try to kill it!

To get you started, here are some sample time-based workouts you might want to try. Keep in mind, the Advanced Level workouts are for elite fighters who have a minimum of 5 years of heavy bag training and conditioning.

Besides the actual body mechanics of punching, there are several other elements that comprise a punching combination. They include attack rhythms, height variations, the cadence of delivery, and practitioner movement.

Sample Time-Based Heavy Bag Workouts

Skill Level	Duration of Each Round	Rest Period	Total Number of rounds
Beginner	1 minute	2 minutes	3
Beginner	1 minute	1 minute	3
Beginner	2 minutes	2 minutes	3
Beginner	2 minutes	1 minute	3
Intermediate	3 minutes	2 minutes	5
Intermediate	3 minutes	1 minute	5
Intermediate	3 minutes	2 minutes	6
Intermediate	3 minutes	1 minute	6
Advanced	4 minutes	2 minutes	8
Advanced	4 minutes	1 minute	8
Advanced	5 minutes	2 minutes	10
Advanced	5 minutes	1 minute	10

All time-based workouts will require you to invest in a workout timer. Luckily, there are dozens of smartphone apps that mimic the same features of an actual interval timer. These workout apps are convenient, inexpensive and can be found at your favorite online app store.

21

What Combinations Should I Throw?

What follows are just a few punching combinations you can perform during your time-based workouts. If you require advanced heavy bag combination training, including step-by-step photographs, please see *Volume 2* of this book series, *Heavy Bag Combinations: The Ultimate Guide to Heavy Bag Punching Combinations.*

Once again, this book assumes you can perform the basic punching skills, including the jab, rear cross, hook, and uppercut. However, if you are not familiar with these foundational techniques, please see the step-by-step instructions featured in the appendix of this book.

When reading the combination sequence on the following pages, please note the word *high* indicates punches delivered at head level and *low* represents punches delivered to the stomach level on the bag.

- Jab (high) - Jab (high)

- Jab (low) - Jab (low)

- Jab (high) - Jab (low)

- Jab (low) - Jab (high)

- Jab (high) - Jab (high) - Rear Cross (high)

- Jab (high) - Jab (high) - Rear Cross (low)

- Jab - Rear Cross (high)

- Jab - Rear Cross (low)

- Jab - Rear Cross (high) - Jab

- Jab - Rear Cross (low) - Jab

- Jab - Rear Cross - Jab - Rear Cross

- Jab - Jab - Rear Cross

- Jab - Rear Cross - Jab

- Jab - Rear Cross - Lead Hook (high)

- Jab - Rear Cross - Lead Hook (low)

- Jab - Rear Cross - Lead Hook (high) - Rear Hook (high)

- Jab - Rear Cross - Lead Hook (low) - Rear Hook (low)

- Jab - Rear Cross - Lead Hook (high) - Rear Hook (low)

- Jab - Rear Cross - Lead Hook (low) - Rear Hook (high)

- Jab - Rear Hook (high)

- Jab - Rear Hook (low)

Heavy Bag Workout

- Jab - Lead Hook (high)
- Jab - Lead Hook (low)
- Jab - Lead Hook (high) - Rear hook (high)
- Jab - Lead Hook (low) - Rear hook (low)
- Jab - Lead Hook (high) - Rear hook (low)
- Jab - Lead Hook (low) - Rear hook (high)
- Jab - Jab - Rear Cross - Lead Hook (high)
- Jab - Jab - Rear Cross - Lead Hook (low)
- Jab - Rear Cross - Lead Hook (high) - Rear Uppercut
- Jab - Rear Cross - Lead Hook (high) - Rear Hook (low) - Lead Uppercut
- Rear Cross - Lead Hook - Lead Hook - Rear Hook (low-high-high-low)
- Rear Cross - Lead Hook - Lead Hook - Rear Hook (high-low-low-high)
- Rear Cross - Lead Hook - Rear Cross - Lead Hook - Rear Hook (high-high-low-high-low)
- Rear Uppercut - Lead Hook (high)
- Rear Uppercut - Lead Hook (low)
- Rear Uppercut - Lead Hook (high) - Rear Hook (high)
- Rear Uppercut - Lead Hook (low) - Rear Hook (low)
- Rear Uppercut - Lead Hook (high) - Rear Hook (low)

Workout Routine #2
Ambidextrous Training

Ambidexterity is the ability to perform with equal facility on both the right and left sides of the body. In simpler terms, it's the capacity to use the right and left hands equally well.

Ambidexterity is a vital attribute for reality-based self-defense training. In fact, it's a regular part of my teaching curriculum. Here are three important reasons why: (1) your strong or dominant hand might be injured in combat, (2) you might be assaulted on the weak side of your body, and (3) your strong hand might be occupied (i.e., holding or carrying an object) during the moment of the assault.

When it comes to high-risk self-defense training, ambidexterity must also be mastered in the following components of combat.

1. Stances -both armed and unarmed combat stances.

2. Submission Holds - including the vertical and horizontal grappling planes.

3. Natural Body Weapons - kicks, punches, and various other striking techniques.

4. Natural Defensive Techniques - blocks, parries, and evasion movements.

5. Knives Fighting

6. Stick Fighting

7. Makeshift Weapons

8. Chemical Irritants

9. Firearm Skills

Ambidexterity for Boxing and Mixed Martial Arts

Ambidexterity is also an invaluable skill for combat sports like boxing, kickboxing, and mixed martial arts. In fact, the ability to fight your opponent from both right (southpaw) and left (orthodox) stances can be advantageous for some of the following reasons.

1. **Opens the opponent up** - Since most boxers are right-handed, they are used to fighting against other right-handed fighters. However, switching from an orthodox to a southpaw stance opens your opponent up to several angular attacks.

2. **Lead hand power & accuracy** - Assuming you are right-handed, switching to a southpaw stance places your most accurate and coordinated hand closer to the opponent. This allows you to jab with greater power and accuracy.

3. **Weak hand power enhancer** - A southpaw stance also brings your weaker left hand back to the rear side of your body. This means greater impact power when delivering rear punches

(i.e., rear cross, hook, and uppercut).

4. **It confuses your opponent** - Finally, switching from an orthodox to a southpaw stance (in the middle if a fight) will undoubtedly confuse the hell out of your opponent and throw off his timing and footwork. In most cases, it will take a couple rounds for him to get his bearing straight. This creates an enormous window of opportunity that you can exploit to your advantage.

Ambidexterity and Heavy Bag Training

There are numerous ways you can incorporate ambidexterity training to your heavy bag workouts. Here are just a few.

1. **Switch after every round** - Begin your first round on the heavy bag from an orthodox (left lead) stance and deliver all of your punching combinations from this position. During the next round, switch to a southpaw (right lead) stance and deliver all of your combinations from this posture. Every round, switch between right and left stances for a total of 8 to

10 rounds.

2. **Switch after every combination** - Deliver a specific combination (i.e., jab-rear cross-lead hook-rear hook) from an orthodox stance. Next, switch to a southpaw stance and perform the same heavy bag combination. Switch back to the orthodox stance and perform another combination. Once again, change to a southpaw stance and deliver the same combination on the bag. Go back and forth between stances for the duration of your round. Perform this for a total of 8 to 10 rounds.

3. **Switch after circling** - From an orthodox stance, deliver a series of combinations while rotating 360-degrees around the bag. Once your circle is complete, switch to a southpaw stance and execute a series of combinations while circling the opposite direction around the bag. Switch back and forth between right and left stances for a total of 8 to 10 rounds.

While many boxing purists will argue against switching stances, there are others who disagree. For example, professional boxers like Marvin Hagler, Michael Moorer, Roy Jones Jr., Manny Pacquiao, and Erik Morales are known for switching their stances during a match.

Ambidextrous Training
Switching Your Stance After Every Round

Round	Stance	Round Duration	Rest Period
1	orthodox	3 minutes	1 minute
2	southpaw	3 minutes	1 minute
3	orthodox	3 minutes	1 minute
4	southpaw	3 minutes	1 minute
5	orthodox	3 minutes	1 minute
6	southpaw	3 minutes	1 minute
7	orthodox	3 minutes	1 minute
8	southpaw	3 minutes	1 minute
9	orthodox	3 minutes	1 minute
10	southpaw	3 minutes	1 minute

Some boxing coaches and trainers will argue that it's too difficult for a fighter to maintain two stances. However, I categorically disagree! As a matter of fact, I've maintained fighting proficiency with both the right and left stances for over 30 years. The bottom line is, if you want something bad enough, you can make it happen!

Switching After Every Combination	
Stance	**Combination Sequence**
orthodox	Jab (high) - Jab (high)
southpaw	Jab (high) - Jab (high)
orthodox	Jab (high) - Jab (low)
southpaw	Jab (high) - Jab (low)
orthodox	Jab (high) - Jab (high) - Rear Cross (low)
southpaw	Jab (high) - Jab (high) - Rear Cross (low)
orthodox	Jab - Rear Cross - Lead Hook (high)
southpaw	Jab - Rear Cross - Lead Hook (high)
orthodox	Jab - Rear Cross - Lead Hook (low) - Rear Hook (low)
southpaw	Jab - Rear Cross - Lead Hook (low) - Rear Hook (low)
orthodox	Jab - Lead Hook (low) - Rear hook (low)
southpaw	Jab - Lead Hook (low) - Rear hook (low)
orthodox	Jab - Jab - Rear Cross - Lead Hook (high)
southpaw	Jab - Jab - Rear Cross - Lead Hook (high)
orthodox	Rear Cross - Lead Hook - Lead Hook - Rear Hook (all high)
southpaw	Rear Cross - Lead Hook - Lead Hook - Rear Hook (all high)

Switching After Circling

Stance	Combination Sequence	Direction of Movement
orthodox	Jab (high) - Jab (high)	Circle left
southpaw	Jab (high) - Jab (high)	Circle right
orthodox	Jab (high) - Jab (low)	Circle left
southpaw	Jab (high) - Jab (low)	Circle right
orthodox	Jab (high) - Jab (high) - Rear Cross (low)	Circle left
southpaw	Jab (high) - Jab (high) - Rear Cross (low)	Circle right
orthodox	Jab - Rear Cross - Lead Hook (high)	Circle left
southpaw	Jab - Rear Cross - Lead Hook (high)	Circle right
orthodox	Jab - Rear Cross - Lead Hook (low) - Rear Hook (low)	Circle left
southpaw	Jab - Rear Cross - Lead Hook (low) - Rear Hook (low)	Circle right
orthodox	Jab - Lead Hook (low) - Rear hook (low)	Circle left
southpaw	Jab - Lead Hook (low) - Rear hook (low)	Circle right
orthodox	Jab - Jab - Rear Cross - Lead Hook (high)	Circle left
southpaw	Jab - Jab - Rear Cross - Lead Hook (high)	Circle right
orthodox	Rear Cross - Lead Hook - Lead Hook - Rear Hook (all high)	Circle left
southpaw	Rear Cross - Lead Hook - Lead Hook - Rear Hook (all high)	Circle right

Workout Routine #3
Elevation Drill

The elevation drill is one of the most demanding exercises you can perform on the heavy bag. Besides requiring a tremendous amount of muscular endurance, the drill also requires a significant amount of mental resilience and attention control.

The objective of this exercise is to keep the heavy bag elevated at a 45-degree angle by continuously punching it. This drill is brutal on the arms. In fact, the average person can barely last 30 seconds. To perform the drill follow these steps:

1. Face the heavy bag and assume a fighting stance.

2. Deliver the jab and rear cross combination continuously. Concentrate on delivering full-speed, full-force punches.

3. Maintain a rapid-fire cadence to keep the bag elevated at a

45-degree angle from the floor.

4. Avoid pushing the bag and remember to snap each blow. If the heavy bag spins when performing this exercise, it means your punches are not landing at the center of the bag. Remember to focus your blows at a single target point.

5. Perform the drill for a minimum of three rounds. Each round can last anywhere from 10 to 90 seconds. If you are exceptionally conditioned, go for 90 seconds.

The goal of the elevation drill is to keep the heavy bag elevated at approximately 45-degrees by continuously punching it.

Be very careful when performing this exercise. One misplaced punch or bent wrist can easily lead to a severe injury.

Elevation Drill Demonstration

Step 1: The practitioner assumes a fighting stance.

Step 2: He begins with a powerful jab.

Step 3: He immediately follows with a rear cross.

Step 4: Next, another powerful jab.

Step 5: The speed and power of the blows elevate the heavy bag at a 45-degree angle.

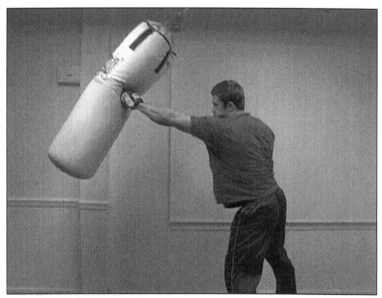

Step 6: To keep the bag elevated at 45-degrees, the practitioner must continue to attack the heavy bag with vicious intent.

Step 7: The practitioner delivers another rapid-fire rear across.

Step 8: Followed by another powerful jab.

Step 9: The practitioner continues his barrage for a total of 60 seconds.

While the elevation drill is designed to be a self-standing workout routine, some boxers will only perform this exercise during the last 10 seconds of a 3 minute heavy bag round.

Elevation Drill Workout Routines

Skill Level	Duration of Each Round	Rest Period	Total Number of rounds
Beginner	10 seconds	2 minutes	3
Beginner	15 seconds	1 minute	3
Beginner	20 seconds	2 minutes	3
Beginner	25 minutes	1 minute	3
Intermediate	30 seconds	2 minutes	5
Intermediate	35 seconds	1 minute	5
Intermediate	40 seconds	2 minutes	5
Intermediate	45 seconds	1 minute	5
Advanced	60 seconds	2 minutes	6
Advanced	70 seconds	1 minute	6
Advanced	80 seconds	2 minutes	6
Advanced	90 seconds	1 minute	6

Workout Routine #4
Piston Punching

Piston Punching is another demanding heavy bag exercise that will push you to your limits. Your objective is to fire off linear blows in a rapid-fire or piston-like fashion *without elevating the bag*. Piston punching can be directed to both high and low heavy bag targets.

Like the elevation drill, this exercise is very taxing on the shoulders, so remember to take your time and gradually increase the intensity of this exercise. To perform piston punching, follow these steps:

1. Face the heavy bag and assume a fighting stance.

2. Deliver the jab and rear cross combination continuously. Concentrate on delivering full-speed, full-force punches.

3. Focus on snapping each punch and *avoid* elevating the bag.

4. If the bag spins when performing this exercise, it means your punches are not landing at the center. Remember to focus all of your blows to a single center point on the bag.

5. Perform the drill for a minimum of three rounds. Each round can last anywhere from 10 to 60 seconds. If you are exceptionally conditioned, go for 90 seconds.

The following photographs demonstrate piston punching at high targets on the heavy bag. Keep in mind that all of these pictures were taken in real-time speed.

Piston Punching Demonstration (high targets only)

Step 1: The drill begins with a powerful jab at the bag.

Step 2: Followed by a rear cross.

Step 3: Next, another powerful jab.

Step 4: The author continues with another rear cross at the bag.

Step 5: He follows up with another jab.

Step 6: Next, another rear cross. Notice how all of his punches are delivered at the center of the bag.

Step 8: Mr. Franco continues his assault for a total of 30 seconds.

Piston Punching Workout Routines

Skill Level	Duration of Each Round	Rest Period	Total Number of rounds
Beginner	10 seconds	2 minutes	3
Beginner	15 seconds	1 minute	3
Beginner	20 seconds	2 minutes	3
Beginner	25 minutes	1 minute	3
Intermediate	30 seconds	2 minutes	5
Intermediate	35 seconds	1 minute	5
Intermediate	40 seconds	2 minutes	5
Intermediate	45 seconds	1 minute	5
Advanced	60 seconds	2 minutes	6
Advanced	70 seconds	1 minute	6
Advanced	80 seconds	2 minutes	6
Advanced	90 seconds	1 minute	6

Workout Routine #5
Cyclone Drill

The Cyclone Drill develops bone-crushing hook punches. The objective of the exercise is to assault the heavy bag with a continuous flurry of hook punches delivered in a back and forth fashion. Like piston punching, this drill permits you to strike both high and low heavy bag targets. To perform the Cyclone drill, follow these steps:

1. Face the heavy bag and assume a fighting stance.

2. Deliver the lead and rear hook punches in a fluid, back and forth fashion. Concentrate on striking the bag as fast and hard as possible.

3. Perform the drill for a minimum of three rounds. Each round can last anywhere from 10 to 90 seconds.

Cyclone Drill Demonstration

Step 1: The practitioner throws a high lead hook punch at the bag.

Step 2: Next, a rear hook.

Step 3: Followed by a lead hook.

Step 4: He continues with a rear hook.

Step 5: Then another high lead hook punch.

Step 6: The practitioner continues his assault for a total of 30 seconds.

Cyclone Drill Workout Routines

Skill Level	Duration of Each Round	Rest Period	Total Number of rounds
Beginner	10 seconds	2 minutes	3
Beginner	15 seconds	1 minute	3
Beginner	20 seconds	2 minutes	3
Beginner	25 minutes	1 minute	3
Intermediate	30 seconds	2 minutes	5
Intermediate	35 seconds	1 minute	5
Intermediate	40 seconds	2 minutes	5
Intermediate	45 seconds	1 minute	5
Advanced	60 seconds	2 minutes	6
Advanced	70 seconds	1 minute	6
Advanced	80 seconds	2 minutes	6
Advanced	90 seconds	1 minute	6

Workout Routine #6
"Hit the Seam" Drill

I developed this unusual exercise approximately 25 years ago. My goal was to design a heavy bag drill that would improve both punching power and accuracy at the same time. As you might already know, the heavy bag is primarily designed for striking power, not target accuracy. However, this drill allows you to simultaneously develop both striking power and target accuracy.

The objective of the drill is to deliberately throw punching combinations at the stitching seam that runs vertically down the heavy bag. This is especially challenging because the heavy bag swings and spins uncontrollably. So you will be forced to move continuously with the bag to ensure proper targeting.

"Hit the seam" also develops target recognition along the opponent's centerline. Essentially, target recognition is the ability to immediately recognize strategic anatomical targets during a fight. Depending on what you are training for (i.e., boxing, mixed martial arts, kickboxing, military combatives, street fighting, etc), the opponent's targets might include his eyes, temple, nose, chin, back of neck, throat, solar plexus, ribs, groin, thighs, knees, and shins.

The Centerline

"Hit the seam" is also ideal for teaching you how to strike the opponent's centerline. The centerline is an imaginary vertical line that divides the opponent's body in half. Located on this line are some of his vital impact targets. This includes the eyes, nose, chin, throat, solar plexus, and groin. Striking these centerline targets in a fight will disrupt your opponent's balance, inhibit his mobility and maximize impact damage. However, keep in mind that combat sports like boxing, mixed martial arts, and kickboxing have rules and regulations that will limit which centerline targets you can strike.

The proper placement of your centerline (in relation to your opponent) is also important and will directly effect your target exposure, balance, mobility, and punching power.

"Hit the Seam" Drill Variations

There are three variations of this drill, and they are listing in order of increased difficulty:

1. Hit the Seam - straight punches only
2. Hit the Seam - circular punches only
3. Hit the Seam - all punches

"Hit the Seam" - Straight Punches Only

This is the easiest of all three variations. It requires you to only throw linear combinations (i.e., jab-jab-rear cross-jab) at the heavy bag seam. Since the heavy bag seam runs vertically down the bag, you can throw both high and low straight punches. Some of them might include the following:

- Jab (high) - Jab (high)

- Jab (low) - Jab (low)

- Jab (high) - Jab (low)

- Jab (low) - Jab (high)

- Jab (high) - Jab (high) - Rear Cross (high)

- Jab (high) - Jab (high) - Rear Cross (low)

- Jab - Rear Cross (high)

- Jab - Rear Cross (low)

- Jab - Rear Cross (high) - Jab

- Jab - Rear Cross (low) - Jab

- Jab - Rear Cross - Jab - Rear Cross

- Jab - Jab - Rear Cross

- Jab - Rear Cross - Jab

"Hit the Seam" - Circular Punches Only

This drill variation requires an intermediate level of heavy bag skill. The goal is to only throw circular punches (hooks, shovel hooks, and uppercuts) at the stitching seam of the heavy bag. Again, since the stitching runs vertically down the bag, you can throw circular punches at both high and low targets. Punching combinations can include some of the following:

- Lead Hook (high) - Rear Hook (high)

- Lead Hook (low) - Lead Hook (low)

- Lead Hook (high) - Rear Hook (low)

- Lead Hook (low) -Rear Hook (high)

- Lead Hook (high) - Lead Hook (high) - Rear Hook (high)

- Lead Hook (high) - Lead Hook (high) - Rear Hook (low)

- Lead Hook (high) - Rear Uppercut (low)

- Lead Hook (high) - - Rear Hook (high) - Rear Uppercut (low)

- Rear Uppercut (low) - Lead Uppercut (low)

- Rear Uppercut (low) - Lead Uppercut (low) - Lead Hook (high) - Rear Hook (high)

- Rear Uppercut (high) - Lead Uppercut (high) - Lead Hook (low) - Rear Hook (low)

"Hit the Seam" - All Punches

This is by far the most challenging of the three variations. It requires you to throw your entire punching arsenal at the seam line. This includes the jab, rear cross, hook, shovel hook, and uppercut. Once again, your punches can be delivered to both high and low heavy bag targets. Some striking combinations can include:

- Jab - Jab- Rear Uppercut (all high)

- Jab - Lead Uppercut - Rear Cross (all high)

- Jab - Lead Uppercut - Rear Cross (low-high-low)

- Jab - Rear Uppercut - Lead Uppercut (all high)

- Jab - Rear Uppercut - Lead Uppercut - Rear Cross - Lead Hook (all high)

- Jab - Rear Cross - Lead Hook - Rear Uppercut (all high)

- Jab - Rear Cross - Lead Hook - Rear Cross (all high)

- Jab - rear cross - Lead Hook - Rear Cross - Lead Hook - Lead Hook (5x high -1 low)

- Rear Cross - Jab - Rear Hook (all high)

- Rear Cross - Jab - Rear Hook -Lead Uppercut - Lead Hook (high-high-low-high-high)

- Rear Cross - Lead Hook - Rear Cross - Lead Hook - Rear Uppercut (high-high-high-low-high)

- Rear Hook - Lead Hook - Rear Hook - Lead Uppercut (all high)

Since the heavy bag seam runs vertically down the bag, you can throw both high and low punching combinations.

"Hit the Seam" Workout Routines

Skill Level	Duration of Each Round	Rest Period	Total Number of rounds
Beginner	1 minute	2 minutes	3
Beginner	1 minute	1 minute	3
Beginner	2 minutes	2 minutes	3
Beginner	2 minutes	1 minute	3
Intermediate	3 minutes	2 minutes	5
Intermediate	3 minutes	1 minute	5
Intermediate	3 minutes	2 minutes	6
Intermediate	3 minutes	1 minute	6
Advanced	4 minutes	2 minutes	8
Advanced	4 minutes	1 minute	8
Advanced	5 minutes	2 minutes	10
Advanced	5 minutes	1 minute	10

If you want to really push yourself, you can combine different routines into a single workout. For example, try combining ambidextrous training with "hit the seam" drill.

Workout Routine #7
X-Training

X-Training is also another methodology that improves both punching power and target accuracy. Compared the previous drill, X-Training is less restrictive. The objective of the exercise is to throw punching combinations at Xs that are on the heavy bag.

Preparing the Bag

The best way to prepare your heavy bag for X-Training is first to cut several small pieces of white electrical tape into two-inch strips. Next, cross two pieces of tape and form an X and press it firmly into the heavy bag. Space the Xs approximately six inches apart from each other and distribute them around the bag. Make certain to place both high and low targets on the bag (see photo).

X-Training Variations

There are three variations of X-Training, and they are listing in order of increased difficulty:

1. X-Training - straight punches only

2. X-Training - circular punches only

3. X-Training - all punches

X-Training works best on leather and vinyl covered heavy bags. Unfortunately, electrical tape won't stick to canvas bags.

Pictured here, a heavy bag prepped for X-Training.

X-Training - Straight Punches Only

This is the easiest of all three variations. It requires you to only throw linear combinations (i.e., jab-jab-rear cross-jab) at the Xs. Some of them might include the following:

- Jab (high) - Jab (high)

- Jab (low) - Jab (low)

- Jab (high) - Jab (low)

- Jab (low) - Jab (high)

- Jab (high) - Jab (high) - Rear Cross (high)

- Jab (high) - Jab (high) - Rear Cross (low)

- Jab - Rear Cross (high)

- Jab - Rear Cross (low)

- Jab - Rear Cross (high) - Jab

- Jab - Rear Cross (low) - Jab

- Jab - Rear Cross - Jab - Rear Cross

- Jab - Jab - Rear Cross

- Jab - Rear Cross - Jab

X-Training - Circular Punches Only

This drill variation requires an intermediate level of heavy bag skill. The goal is to only throw circular punches (hooks, shovel hooks, and uppercuts) at the white targets. Punching combinations can include some of the following:

- Lead Hook (high) - Rear Hook (high)

- Lead Hook (low) - Lead Hook (low)

- Lead Hook (high) - Rear Hook (low)

- Lead Hook (low) -Rear Hook (high)

- Lead Hook (high) - Lead Hook (high) - Rear Hook (high)

- Lead Hook (high) - Lead Hook (high) - Rear Hook (low)

- Lead Hook (high) - Rear Uppercut (low)

- Lead Hook (high) - - Rear Hook (high) - Rear Uppercut (low)

- Rear Uppercut (low) - Lead Uppercut (low)

- Rear Uppercut (low) - Lead Uppercut (low) - Lead Hook (high) - Rear Hook (high)

- Rear Uppercut (high) - Lead Uppercut (high) - Lead Hook (low) - Rear Hook (low)

X-Training - All Punches

This is the most challenging of the three variations. It requires you to throw your entire punching arsenal at the Xs. This includes the jab, rear cross, hook, shovel hook, and uppercut. Once again, your punches can be delivered to both high and low heavy bag targets. Some striking combinations can include:

- Jab - Jab- Rear Uppercut (all high)

- Jab - Lead Uppercut - Rear Cross (all high)

- Jab - Lead Uppercut - Rear Cross (low-high-low)

Heavy Bag Workout

- Jab - Rear Uppercut - Lead Uppercut (all high)

- Jab - Rear Uppercut - Lead Uppercut - Rear Cross - Lead Hook (all high)

- Jab - Rear Cross - Lead Hook - Rear Uppercut (all high)

- Jab - Rear Cross - Lead Hook - Rear Cross (all high)

- Jab - rear cross - Lead Hook - Rear Cross - Lead Hook - Lead Hook (5x high -1 low)

- Rear Cross - Jab - Rear Hook (all high)

- Rear Cross - Jab - Rear Hook -Lead Uppercut - Lead Hook (high-high-low-high-high)

- Rear Cross - Lead Hook - Rear Cross - Lead Hook - Rear Uppercut (high-high-high-low-high)

- Rear Hook - Lead Hook - Rear Hook - Lead Uppercut (all high)

If you are training for a competitive match, always workout on the bag with a mouthpiece in your mouth. Remember, train the way you will fight and fight the way you train!

X-Training Workout Routines

Skill Level	Duration of Each Round	Rest Period	Total Number of rounds
Beginner	1 minute	2 minutes	3
Beginner	1 minute	1 minute	3
Beginner	2 minutes	2 minutes	3
Beginner	2 minutes	1 minute	3
Intermediate	3 minutes	2 minutes	5
Intermediate	3 minutes	1 minute	5
Intermediate	3 minutes	2 minutes	6
Intermediate	3 minutes	1 minute	6
Advanced	4 minutes	2 minutes	8
Advanced	4 minutes	1 minute	8
Advanced	5 minutes	2 minutes	10
Advanced	5 minutes	1 minute	10

Learn to relax and avoid tensing your muscles when throwing combinations. Muscular tension will throw off your timing, retard the speed of your punches, and wear you out during a round.

Workout Routine #8
"Punch-a Hole" Exercise

Any boxer worth his salt will tell you that heavy bag training is a delicate mixture of power, speed, timing, and pacing. However, the real secret to making it through a full three-minute round on the heavy bag is to pace the power of your strikes.

Some of you might already know that full force, full speed punching will invariably lead to a very short-lived training round. In most instances, the average person can only sustain "all out" power punching for approximately 30 seconds. That's also assuming they are punching with proper form.

The "Punch a Hole" exercise goes against this conventional wisdom by training you to hit the bag as hard as humanly possible. In essence, your goal is to literally try and punch a hole through the heavy bag. Is this actually possible? I seriously doubt it! Nevertheless, this type of training will transform your fists into sledgehammers.

"Punch a Hole" Workout Demonstration

Step 1: The practitioner assumes a fighting stance.

Step 2: He throws a rear cross punch.

Step 3: Next, he follows up with a strong jab.

Step 4: He drives a powerful low rear uppercut.

Step 5: A high lead hook punch.

Step 6: Followed by a bone-shattering rear cross.

Step 7: Another explosive jab.

Step 8: The practitioner continues his assault for a total of 30 seconds.

Beginner Level
"Punch a Hole" Workout Routines

Workout Routine	Duration of Each Round	Rest Period	Total Number of rounds
1	10 seconds	2 minutes	3
2	10 seconds	1 minute	3
3	15 seconds	2 minutes	3
4	15 seconds	1 minute	3
5	20 seconds	2 minutes	3
6	20 seconds	1 minute	3
7	25 seconds	2 minutes	3
8	25 seconds	1 minute	3
9	10 seconds	1 minute	5
10	15 seconds	2 minutes	5
11	20 seconds	1 minute	5
12	25 seconds	2 minutes	5

The "punch a hole" drill requires you to hit the bag as hard as possible! Do not perform this exercise unless you are absolutely certain you have mastered the proper body mechanics of punching.

Intermediate Level "Punch a Hole" Workout Routines			
Workout Routine	**Duration of Each Round**	**Rest Period**	**Total Number of rounds**
1	30 seconds	2 minutes	3
2	30 seconds	1 minute	3
3	35 seconds	2 minutes	3
4	35 seconds	1 minute	3
5	40 seconds	2 minutes	3
6	40 seconds	1 minute	3
7	45 seconds	2 minutes	3
8	45 seconds	1 minute	3
9	30 seconds	1 minute	5
10	35 seconds	2 minutes	5
11	40 seconds	1 minute	5
12	45 seconds	2 minutes	5

Performing this drill for a duration of 30-45 seconds might not seem like a lot. However, I can assure you that after 5 rounds you will be thoroughly exhausted.

Advanced Level
"Punch a Hole" Workout Routines

Workout Routine	Duration of Each Round	Rest Period	Total Number of rounds
1	50 seconds	2 minutes	4
2	50 seconds	1 minute	4
3	55 seconds	2 minutes	4
4	55 seconds	1 minute	4
5	60 seconds	2 minutes	5
6	60 seconds	1 minute	5
7	65 seconds	2 minutes	5
8	65 seconds	1 minute	5
9	50 seconds	1 minute	6
10	55 seconds	2 minutes	6
11	60 seconds	1 minute	6
12	65 seconds	2 minutes	6

Performing this drill for a duration of 60 seconds or longer is generally reserved for professional fighters who want peak combat performance.

Workout Routine #9
Technique Isolation Training

Technique Isolation training is a variation of my proficiency training methodology. The purpose of this exercise is to focus exclusively on one punch (i.e., jab, rear cross, lead hook, etc.) for your entire workout. For example, if you wanted to sharpen and develop your jab, you would isolate and practice it exclusively on the heavy bag for a specified number of rounds.

"I fear not the man who has practiced 10,000 kicks once, but I fear the man who has practiced one kick 10,000 times."

-Bruce Lee

Isolation Training (Jab) Demonstration

Step 1: The practitioner assumes a stance.

Step 2: He delivers a high left jab.

Step 3: He begins circling the bag in a clockwise direction.

Step 4: He throws a low jab

Step 5: As he moves around the bag, he throws another high jab.

Step 6: Next, another low jab.

Step 7: Followed by a high jab.

Step 8: He delivers another low jab and continues to circle around the heavy bag.

Step 9: He fires off another high jab.

Step 10: The practitioner continues jabbing and moving around the at the bag for a duration of 3 minutes.

Technique Isolation Workout Routines

Skill Level	Duration of Each Round	Rest Period	Total Number of rounds
Beginner	1 minute	2 minutes	3
Beginner	1 minute	1 minute	3
Beginner	2 minutes	2 minutes	3
Beginner	2 minutes	1 minute	3
Intermediate	3 minutes	2 minutes	5
Intermediate	3 minutes	1 minute	5
Intermediate	3 minutes	2 minutes	6
Intermediate	3 minutes	1 minute	6
Advanced	4 minutes	2 minutes	8
Advanced	4 minutes	1 minute	8
Advanced	5 minutes	2 minutes	10
Advanced	5 minutes	1 minute	10

In order to maximize the full benefit of technique isolation training, it's important to stick to only one punch for your entire workout. For example, if you're a beginner who wants to perfect your jab, you would practice it exclusively for a total of 3 rounds.

Workout Routine #10
Defensive Bag Training

Heavy bag training isn't just about offense. In fact, there are several drills designed to sharpen your defensive techniques and improve your defensive reaction time.

A good defensive structure requires mastery of the following four tools: blocks, parries, slipping, and footwork. I can say without reservation that all of these defensive techniques work effectively against boxers, street brawlers, and martial artists of all styles and backgrounds. However, before I can discuss the specific defensive tools, it's important to talk about defensive reaction time when fighting.

What is Defensive Reaction Time?

Defensive reaction time is defined as the elapsed time between the opponent's attack (e.g., jab, hook, rear cross) and your defensive response to that attack (e.g., block, parry, evasion movement). Your defensive reaction time is the result of three fluid stages (defensive recognition, defensive selection, and defensive execution).

1. ***Defensive recognition*** is the first stage where you recognize and identify that an attack has occurred.
2. ***Defensive selection*** is the second stage where you immediately select the appropriate defensive tool, technique, or response.
3. ***Defensive execution*** is the third and final phase where your body performs the appropriate defensive tool, technique, or response.

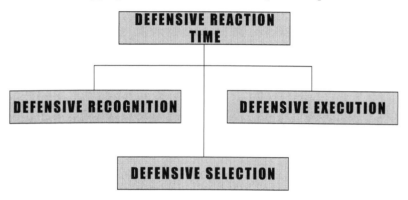

Defensive reaction time is the result of three fluid stages: defensive recognition, defensive selection, and defensive execution.

How To Minimize Defensive Reaction Time

When it comes to fighting (including both sport and street), your objective is to minimize your defensive reaction time as much as possible. Luckily, there are several ways to accomplish this.

First, try to be able to read advance information about the opponent's attack. This is referred to as *telegraphic cognizance*. For example, when your opponent chambers his arm back prior to delivering a punch.

Second, limit your number of defensive responses to a particular type of attack. For example, if your opponent attacks with a jab to your head, you should have only *one specific* defensive response programmed. In this instance, you would parry or deflect the threatening blow.

Third, all of your defensive responses should be natural and performed in a simple fashion. Again, in the case of the jab, not only would you execute a horizontal parry, but you would also situate it on the same side of the opponent's attack (this is called mirror-image parrying).

Fourth, practice, practice, practice! Your defensive responses must be practiced over and over again until they become second nature. Sparring, shadowboxing, focus mitt drills, and even heavy bag training will help you develop these important skills.

Before we get into the defensive heavy bag exercise, let's review all of the different defensive techniques you would use in a fight.

Arm Blocks

Blocks are defensive techniques designed to intercept your assailant's circular attacks. Blocks are executed by placing a non vital body part between the opponent's strike and your body target. There are three primary blocks with which you need to be proficient. They include high blocks, mid-blocks, and elbow blocks.

Never forget that offense is only half the game. Defensive skills are just as important and they must be practiced frequently to ensure that you will survive in the streets as well as the ring.

High Block

The high block is primarily used for street self-defense and it's designed to protect you against overhead blows. To execute the lead high block, simply raise your lead arm up and extend your forearm out and above your head. Be careful not to position your arm where your head is exposed. Make certain that your hand is open and not clenched. This will increase the surface area of your block and provide a quick counterattack. The mechanics for the lead high block are the same as for the rear high block. Raise your rear arm up and extend your forearm out and above your head.

The high block.

Mid-Block

The mid-block is used to defend against circular blows to your head or upper torso. To perform the block, raise either your right or left arm at approximately 90 degrees while simultaneously pronating (rotating) it into the direction of the strike. Make contact with the belly of your forearm at the assailant's wrist or forearm. This movement will provide maximum structural integrity for the blocking tool. Make certain that your hand is held open to increase the surface area of your block.

The mid block.

Elbow Block

The elbow block is frequently used in boxing, kickboxing, and mixed martial arts. It's designed to stop circular blows to your midsection, such as uppercuts, shovel hooks, and even hook kicks. To execute the elbow block, drop your elbow and simultaneously twist your body toward your centerline. Be certain to keep your elbow perpendicular to the floor and keep your hands relaxed and close to your chest. The elbow block can be used on both the right and left sides.

The elbow block.

Hand Parries

The parry is a quick, forceful slap that picks-off and redirects your assailant's linear strike (i.e., jab, and rear cross). There are two general types of parries, horizontal and vertical, and both can be executed with the right and left hands.

Horizontal Parry

To properly execute a horizontal parry from a fighting stance, move your lead hand horizontally across your body (centerline) to deflect and redirect the assailant's punch. Immediately return to your guard position. Be certain to make contact with the palm of your hand. With sufficient training, you can effectively incorporate the horizontal parry into slipping maneuvers.

Pictured here, the horizontal parry.

Vertical Parry

To execute a vertical parry, from a fighting stance, move your hand vertically down your body (centerline) to deflect and redirect the assailant's blow. Once again, don't forget to counterattack your assailant. **CAUTION:** *Do not parry with your fingers. The fingers provide no structural integrity, and they can be jammed or broken easily.*

Slipping

Slipping is a quick defensive maneuver that permits you to avoid an assailant's linear blow (e.g., jab, rear cross) without stepping out of range. Safe and effective slipping requires precise timing and is accomplished by quickly snapping the head and upper torso sideways (right or left) or backward to avoid the oncoming blow. One of the greatest advantages to slipping is that it frees your hands so that you can simultaneously counter your attacker. There are three ways to slip: right, left, and back.

Slipping requires precise timing.

Slipping Right

Begin from a fighting stance and quickly sway your head and upper torso to the right to avoid the assailant's blow. Quickly counterpunch or return to the starting position.

Slipping Left

Start from a fighting stance and quickly sway your head and upper torso to the left to avoid the assailant's linear blow. Quickly counterpunch or return to the starting position.

Slipping Back (or the Snap Back)

Begin from a fighting stance and quickly snap your head back enough to avoid being hit. Quickly counter or return to the starting position.

Footwork

The final component of defense is footwork. In defense, footwork allows you to disengage quickly from the range of attack and quickly re-engage with an effective counterattack.

Footwork facilitates mobility and it's imperative that you constantly move during the course of a fight. Mobility is critical because it makes it difficult for your opponent to hit you, while at the same time enhancing the power of your strikes.

Mobility is defined as your ability to move your body quickly and economically. This can be accomplished through basic footwork. The safest footwork involves quick, economical steps performed on the balls of your feet, while you remain relaxed and balanced.

Basic Footwork Movements

Basic footwork can be used for both offensive and defensive purposes, and it is structured around four general directions: advancing, retreating, sidestepping right, and sidestepping left.

Moving Forward (Advancing)

From your fighting stance, first move your front foot forward (approximately 18 to 24 inches) and then move your rear foot an equal distance.

Moving Backward (Retreating)

From your fighting stance, first move your rear foot backward (approximately 18 to 24 inches) and then move your front foot an equal distance.

Moving Right (Sidestepping Right)

From a fighting stance, first move your right foot to the right (approximately 18 to 24 inches) and then move your left foot an equal distance.

Moving Left (Sidestepping Left)

From a fighting stance, first move your left foot to the left (approximately 18 to 24 inches) and then move your left foot an equal distance.

Practice these four movements every day for 10 to 15 minutes in front of a full-length mirror until your footwork is quick, balanced, and natural.

The mirror is the best tool for developing quick footwork skills.

Advanced Footwork

Once you have mastered basic footwork, you can incorporate strategic circling into your cache of techniques. Strategic circling is an advanced form of footwork where the fighter uses his lead leg as a pivot point. This advanced footwork can be used defensively to evade an overwhelming assault or offensively to strike the enemy from a strategic angle. Strategic circling can be performed from either a right or left stance.

Circling Right (from a Southpaw Stance)

This means you'll be moving your body around the heavy bag in a counterclockwise direction From a right stance, step 8 to 12 inches to the right with your right foot, then use your right leg as a pivot point and wheel your entire rear leg to the right until the correct stance and positioning is acquired.

Circling Left (from an Orthodox Stance)

This means you'll be moving your body around the heavy bag in a clockwise direction. From a left stance, step 8 to 12 inches to the left with your left foot, then use your left leg as a pivot point and wheel your entire rear leg to the left until the correct stance and positioning is acquired.

Don't forget! You can significantly reduce defensive reaction time by applying some of the following strategies: (1) Recognize advance information about your opponent's attack. (2) Limit your number of defensive options to a particular attack. (3) Make your defensive response natural and simple. (4) Practice, practice, practice!

Sidestep Heavy Bag Drill (with a partner)

Now that we covered all of the defensive techniques it's time to teach you a few defensive oriented heavy bag drills. Let's start with the sidestep drill.

This drill is important for developing evasion skills and for enhancing your sense of range and timing. You'll need a training partner to perform this exercise. To practice the sidestepping drill, employ the following:

1. Face the heavy bag and assume a stance.

2. You training partner holds the heavy bag as you throw punching combinations.

3. At the ideal moment, your training partner forcefully pushes the bag at you.

4. Quickly sidestep away from the bag. If you're standing in a southpaw stance, quickly step with your right foot to the right and move your left leg an equal distance. If you're standing in an orthodox stance, quickly step with your left foot to the left and have your right leg follow an equal distance. When performed correctly, the heavy bag should miss you.

5. Next, your training partner gains control of the swinging bag and you resume throwing combinations.

6. Perform the drill for a minimum of three rounds. Each round can last anywhere from two to five minutes.

Holding the Heavy Bag

There are two different ways your training partner can hold the bag for you when performing defensive bag drills.

Pictured here, the close-up holding position.

The extended holding position.

Sidestep Drill Workout Routines (with a partner)

Skill Level	Duration of Each Round	Rest Period	Total Number of rounds
Beginner	1 minute	2 minutes	3
Beginner	1 minute	1 minute	3
Beginner	2 minutes	2 minutes	3
Beginner	2 minutes	1 minute	3
Intermediate	3 minutes	2 minutes	5
Intermediate	3 minutes	1 minute	5
Intermediate	3 minutes	2 minutes	6
Intermediate	3 minutes	1 minute	6
Advanced	4 minutes	2 minutes	8
Advanced	4 minutes	1 minute	8
Advanced	5 minutes	2 minutes	10
Advanced	5 minutes	1 minute	10

Defensive competency requires you to be adequately prepared to defend against a myriad of adversaries, including poorly skilled opponents. For example, you must be capable of defending against a tight boxer's hook as well as a sloppy, awkward haymaker.

Sidestep Heavy Bag Drill (solo practice)

This is a variation of the sidestep partner drill. Once again, this defensive exercise develops both footwork and timing skills. To perform the exercise, employ the following steps:

1. Face the heavy bag and assume a fighting stance.

2. Begin throwing combinations at the bag.

3. After you complete a few combinations, forcefully push the bag in front of you.

4. When the bags swings back at you, quickly sidestep. If you're standing in a southpaw stance, quickly step with your right foot to the right and have your left leg follow an equal distance. If you're standing in an orthodox stance, quickly step with your left foot to the left and have your right leg follow an equal distance. When performed correctly, the heavy bag should miss you.

5. Reposition yourself and resume throwing combinations at the swinging bag.

6. Perform the drill for a minimum of three rounds. Each round can last anywhere from two to five minutes.

Rope skipping is another effective way of improving your footwork skills. It can be performed as an independent workout or added to your heavy bag routine. Please see the section on interval training for more information.

Sidestep Drill Workout Routines (solo training)

Skill Level	Duration of Each Round	Rest Period	Total Number of rounds
Beginner	1 minute	2 minutes	3
Beginner	1 minute	1 minute	3
Beginner	2 minutes	2 minutes	3
Beginner	2 minutes	1 minute	3
Intermediate	3 minutes	2 minutes	5
Intermediate	3 minutes	1 minute	5
Intermediate	3 minutes	2 minutes	6
Intermediate	3 minutes	1 minute	6
Advanced	4 minutes	2 minutes	8
Advanced	4 minutes	1 minute	8
Advanced	5 minutes	2 minutes	10
Advanced	5 minutes	1 minute	10

A good defensive structure is predicated on a stance that minimizes target exposure, facilitates balance and mobility, and permits quick and evasive movement.

Circling Heavy Bag Drill (with a partner)

This circling drill is another defensive exercise that develops both footwork and counterpunching skills. Once again, you'll need a training partner to perform this exercise. To practice the circling drill, employ the following steps:

1. Face the heavy bag and assume a fighting stance.

2. You training holds the heavy bag while you begin throwing various punching combinations.

3. At the ideal moment, your partner forcefully pushes the bag at you.

4. Quickly circle away from the bag. If you're standing in a southpaw stance, quickly step eight to twelve inches to the right with your right foot, and then use your right leg as a pivot point and wheel your entire rear leg to the right until the correct stance and positioning are acquired. If you're standing in an orthodox stance, quickly step eight to twelve inches to the left with your left foot and then use your left leg as a pivot point and wheel your entire rear leg to the left until the correct stance and positioning are acquired. When performed correctly, the heavy bag should miss you.

5. While simultaneously circling, throw a counterpunch at the swinging bag. The punch you choose will be dependent on a few factors, such as the distance of the target and angle of your body.

6. Perform the drill for a minimum of three rounds. Each round can last anywhere from two to five minutes.

Circling Drill Workout Routines (with a partner)

Skill Level	Duration of Each Round	Rest Period	Total Number of rounds
Beginner	1 minute	2 minutes	3
Beginner	1 minute	1 minute	3
Beginner	2 minutes	2 minutes	3
Beginner	2 minutes	1 minute	3
Intermediate	3 minutes	2 minutes	5
Intermediate	3 minutes	1 minute	5
Intermediate	3 minutes	2 minutes	6
Intermediate	3 minutes	1 minute	6
Advanced	4 minutes	2 minutes	8
Advanced	4 minutes	1 minute	8
Advanced	5 minutes	2 minutes	10
Advanced	5 minutes	1 minute	10

When working out on the bag, always be aware of your chin placement. Remember to always keep your chin angled slightly down. This makes you a more elusive target and help minimize direct strikes to your chin and nose. However, avoid forcing your chin down too low. This will inhibit the fluidity of your punches and ultimately slow you down.

Circling Heavy Bag Drill (solo practice)

This is a variation of the partner drill. Once again, this defensive exercise develops both footwork and counterpunching skills. To perform the exercise, employ the following steps:

1. Face the heavy bag and assume a fighting stance.

2. Begin throwing combinations at the heavy bag.

3. After a few combinations, push the bag in front of you.

4. When the bag swings back at you, circle away from it. If you're standing in a right (southpaw) stance, quickly step eight to twelve inches to the right with your right foot, and then use your right leg as a pivot point and wheel your entire rear leg to the right until the correct stance and positioning are acquired. If you're standing in a left (orthodox) stance, quickly step eight to twelve inches to the left with your left foot and then use your left leg as a pivot point and wheel your entire rear leg to the left until the correct stance and positioning are acquired. When performed correctly, the heavy bag should miss you.

5. While simultaneously circling, throw a counterpunch at the heavy bag. Again, the punch you choose will be dependent on the distance of the bag and angle of your body.

6. Perform the drill for a minimum of three rounds. Each round can last anywhere from two to five minutes.

	Circling Drill Workout Routines (solo training)		
Skill Level	Duration of Each Round	Rest Period	Total Number of rounds
Beginner	1 minute	2 minutes	3
Beginner	1 minute	1 minute	3
Beginner	2 minutes	2 minutes	3
Beginner	2 minutes	1 minute	3
Intermediate	3 minutes	2 minutes	5
Intermediate	3 minutes	1 minute	5
Intermediate	3 minutes	2 minutes	6
Intermediate	3 minutes	1 minute	6
Advanced	4 minutes	2 minutes	8
Advanced	4 minutes	1 minute	8
Advanced	5 minutes	2 minutes	10
Advanced	5 minutes	1 minute	10

When moving around the heavy bag, try to maintain a 50-percent weight distribution. This "noncommittal" weight distribution will provide you with the ability to move in any direction quickly and efficiently, while also supplying you with the necessary stability to withstand and defend against various blows.

99

Slipping Heavy Bag Drill (solo practice)

This is another defensive drill that works on both your slipping and snapback skills. To perform the exercise, employ the following steps:

1. Face the heavy bag and assume a fighting stance.

2. Begin throwing combinations at the bag.

3. After you complete a few combinations, arbitrarily slip your head and body to the side. Try to visualize the opponent's punch coming at you. Remember, it's important that your mental images are clear, strong, and consistent.

4. Return to the stance position and resume punching.

5. Perform the drill for a minimum of three rounds. Each round can last anywhere from two to five minutes.

One of the most important elements of heavy bag training is stability. If stability is compromised, then so is your stance. Here are three principles to keep in mind when trying to achieve stability in your stance: (1) keeping your center of gravity directly over your feet, (2) the lower you drop your center of gravity to its support base, the greater stability you will have, (3) the wider your stance, the greater your stability.

Slipping Drill Workout Routines (solo training)			
Skill Level	Duration of Each Round	Rest Period	Total Number of rounds
Beginner	1 minute	2 minutes	3
Beginner	1 minute	1 minute	3
Beginner	2 minutes	2 minutes	3
Beginner	2 minutes	1 minute	3
Intermediate	3 minutes	2 minutes	5
Intermediate	3 minutes	1 minute	5
Intermediate	3 minutes	2 minutes	6
Intermediate	3 minutes	1 minute	6
Advanced	4 minutes	2 minutes	8
Advanced	4 minutes	1 minute	8
Advanced	5 minutes	2 minutes	10
Advanced	5 minutes	1 minute	10

Slipping can be performed while simultaneously counter punching the opponent. It can also be used in conjunction with parring.

Workout Routine #11
Interval Training

Heavy Bag interval training requires you to alternate between two different activities throughout your workout. For our purposes, we are going to integrate five different activities with the heavy bag. They are:

1. Rope skipping
2. Shadowboxing
3. Double-end bag training
4. Focus mitt training
5. Speed bag training

Rope Skipping Integration

If you want to be quick and light on your feet, you will need to jump rope on a regular basis. Jumping rope is also one of the most effective ways of conditioning your heart and improving coordination, endurance, balance, agility, and body composition.

Fortunately, you can integrate rope skipping into your heavy bag routine. However, one of the most important factors to consider when selecting a rope is the length. A simple method to measure the rope properly is to stand on the center of the rope with one foot. The handles of the rope should reach your armpits.

Interval training with the jump rope requires you to alternate exercises after every round. For example, your first round would include heavy bag training, followed by a round of skipping rope, then heavy bag training, and so on.

What follows are some interval workout routines featuring heavy bag training and rope skipping. For your convenience, I have included beginner, intermediate, and advanced workout programs.

Beginner Level Interval Workout Routine (Skipping Rope)			
Round	Activity	Duration of Each Round	Rest Period
1	Heavy Bag	1 minute	2 minutes
2	Jump Rope	2 minutes	1 minute
3	Heavy Bag	2 minutes	2 minutes
4	Jump Rope	1 minute	1 minute
5	Heavy Bag	2 minutes	2 minutes
6	Jump Rope	2 minutes	1 minute
7	Heavy Bag	1 minute	2 minutes
8	Jump Rope	1 minute	1 minute

	Intermediate Level Interval Workout Routine (Skipping Rope)		
Round	Activity	Duration of Each Round	Rest Period
1	Heavy Bag	2 minutes	2 minutes
2	Jump Rope	2 minutes	1 minute
3	Heavy Bag	2 minutes	2 minutes
4	Jump Rope	2 minutes	1 minute
5	Heavy Bag	2 minutes	2 minutes
6	Jump Rope	2 minutes	1 minute
7	Heavy Bag	2 minutes	2 minutes
8	Jump Rope	2 minutes	1 minute
9	Heavy Bag	2 minutes	2 minutes
10	Jump Rope	2 minutes	2 minutes

Learning how to skip rope can be very frustrating. Learn to be patient and the skill will come to you. It just takes time!

Advanced Level
Interval Workout Routine (Skipping Rope)

Round	Activity	Duration of Each Round	Rest Period
1	Heavy Bag	2 minutes	2 minutes
2	Jump Rope	2 minutes	1 minute
3	Heavy Bag	3 minutes	2 minutes
4	Jump Rope	3 minutes	1 minute
5	Heavy Bag	3 minutes	2 minutes
6	Jump Rope	3 minutes	1 minute
7	Heavy Bag	3 minutes	2 minutes
8	Jump Rope	3 minutes	1 minute
9	Heavy Bag	3 minutes	2 minutes
10	Jump Rope	3 minutes	2 minutes
11	Heavy Bag	3 minutes	2 minutes
12	Jump Rope	3 minutes	2 minutes

If you're not careful, you can develop shin splints from skipping rope on hard surfaces like concrete and asphalt. If possible, try to jump rope on a flexible surface like a rubber mat.

Rope Skipping Guidelines

Here are some other guidelines that will help you when skipping rope:

1. Relax your arms and shoulders when jumping.

2. Push off your toes and land gently on the balls of your feet.

3. Use your wrists and forearms to turn the rope, not your shoulders.

4. Maintain good posture and bend naturally at the knees and hips.

5. Jump low, approximately one inch off the ground.

6. Keep your head up and avoid the tendency to look down at your feet.

7. Keep both elbows close to your sides.

8. Avoid jumping rope barefoot.

9. Don't get frustrated by a tangled rope, it's part of the learning process.

10. Jump to different types of music and discover what tunes work best for you.

Shadowboxing Integration

Shadowboxing is the creative deployment of offensive and defensive techniques and maneuvers against an imaginary opponent. It requires intense mental concentration, honest self-analysis, and a deep commitment to improve.

For someone on a tight budget, the good news is that shadowboxing is inexpensive. All you need is a full-length mirror and a place to work out. The mirror is vital. It functions as a critic, your personal instructor. If you're honest, the mirror will be too. It will point out every mistake - telegraphing, sloppy footwork, poor body mechanics, and even lack of physical conditioning.

Proper shadowboxing develops speed, power, balance, footwork, combination skills, sound form, and finesse. It even promotes a better understanding of the ranges of combat.

As you progress, you can incorporate light dumbbells into shadowboxing workouts to enhance power and speed. Start off with one to three pounds and gradually work your way up.

Once again, interval training with shadowboxing requires you to alternate drills after every round. For example, your first round would include heavy bag training, followed by a round of shadowboxing, then heavy bag training, and so on.

What follows are a few interval workout routines featuring heavy bag training and shadowboxing.

Heavy Bag Workout

	Beginner Level Interval Workout Routine (Shadowboxing)		
Round	Activity	Duration of Each Round	Rest Period
1	Heavy Bag	1 minute	2 minutes
2	Shadowboxing	2 minutes	1 minute
3	Heavy Bag	2 minutes	2 minutes
4	Shadowboxing	1 minute	1 minute
5	Heavy Bag	2 minutes	2 minutes
6	Shadowboxing	2 minutes	1 minute
7	Heavy Bag	1 minute	2 minutes
8	Shadowboxing	1 minute	1 minute

Intermediate Level Interval Workout Routine (Shadowboxing)			
Round	Activity	Duration of Each Round	Rest Period
1	Heavy Bag	2 minutes	2 minutes
2	Shadowboxing	2 minutes	1 minute
3	Heavy Bag	2 minutes	2 minutes
4	Shadowboxing	2 minutes	1 minute
5	Heavy Bag	2 minutes	2 minutes
6	Shadowboxing	2 minutes	1 minute
7	Heavy Bag	2 minutes	2 minutes
8	Shadowboxing	2 minutes	1 minute
9	Heavy Bag	2 minutes	2 minutes
10	Shadowboxing	2 minutes	2 minutes

Heavy Bag Workout

	Advanced Level		
	Interval Workout Routine (Shadowboxing)		
Round	**Activity**	**Duration of Each Round**	**Rest Period**
1	Heavy Bag	2 minutes	2 minutes
2	Shadowboxing	2 minutes	1 minute
3	Heavy Bag	3 minutes	2 minutes
4	Shadowboxing	3 minutes	1 minute
5	Heavy Bag	3 minutes	2 minutes
6	Shadowboxing	3 minutes	1 minute
7	Heavy Bag	3 minutes	2 minutes
8	Shadowboxing	3 minutes	1 minute
9	Heavy Bag	3 minutes	2 minutes
10	Shadowboxing	3 minutes	2 minutes
11	Heavy Bag	3 minutes	2 minutes
12	Shadowboxing	3 minutes	2 minutes

If you really want to challenge yourself, consider shadowboxing with a weight vest. This will strengthen your entire body, including your cardiovascular system.

Double-End Bag Integration

The double-end bag is a small, inflatable lightweight bag constructed of vinyl or leather. It is suspended in the air using a durable elastic bungee cord that anchors it to the ceiling and the floor.

This unique piece of equipment allows you to develop both offensive and defensive fighting skills. What follows is a brief list a fighting attributes that can be developed:

- Improves punching accuracy.

- Improves offensive timing.

- Improves punching speed.

- Improves eye-hand coordination.

- Develops counterpunching skills.

- Develops defensive techniques such as slipping skills.

- Improves reflexes.

- Develops cardiovascular endurance

- Develops punching endurance.

- Develops punching combination skills.

The double-end bag also comes in three different sizes including large, medium and small. The smaller the bag, the more challenging it is to hit. As a rule of thumb, beginners should always start off with a large size bag.

Heavy Bag Workout

Here are a few interval workout routines featuring both the heavy bag and double-end bag.

Beginner Level Interval Workout Routine (Double-end bag)			
Round	Activity	Duration of Each Round	Rest Period
1	Heavy Bag	1 minute	2 minutes
2	Double-end bag	2 minutes	1 minute
3	Heavy Bag	2 minutes	2 minutes
4	Double-end bag	1 minute	1 minute
5	Heavy Bag	2 minutes	2 minutes
6	Double-end bag	2 minutes	1 minute
7	Heavy Bag	1 minute	2 minutes
8	Double-end bag	1 minute	1 minute

Intermediate Level Interval Workout Routine (Double-end bag)			
Round	Activity	Duration of Each Round	Rest Period
1	Heavy Bag	2 minutes	2 minutes
2	Double-end bag	2 minutes	1 minute
3	Heavy Bag	2 minutes	2 minutes
4	Double-end bag	2 minutes	1 minute
5	Heavy Bag	2 minutes	2 minutes
6	Double-end bag	2 minutes	1 minute
7	Heavy Bag	2 minutes	2 minutes
8	Double-end bag	2 minutes	1 minute
9	Heavy Bag	2 minutes	2 minutes
10	Double-end bag	2 minutes	2 minutes

The double-end bag requires considerable practice and a lot of patience. In fact, it is probably one of the most difficult pieces of training equipment to master.

	Advanced Level Interval Workout Routine (Double-end-bag)		
Round	Activity	Duration of Each Round	Rest Period
1	Heavy Bag	2 minutes	2 minutes
2	Double-end bag	2 minutes	1 minute
3	Heavy Bag	3 minutes	2 minutes
4	Double-end bag	3 minutes	1 minute
5	Heavy Bag	3 minutes	2 minutes
6	Double-end bag	3 minutes	1 minute
7	Heavy Bag	3 minutes	2 minutes
8	Double-end bag	3 minutes	1 minute
9	Heavy Bag	3 minutes	2 minutes
10	Double-end bag	3 minutes	2 minutes
11	Heavy Bag	3 minutes	2 minutes
12	Double-end bag	3 minutes	2 minutes

To properly control the movement of the double-end bag, you must always hit it directly in the center. If you don't it will bounce uncontrollably to the right and left.

Focus Mitt Integration

The focus mitt (or punching mitt) is an exceptional piece of equipment that can be used by just about anyone. It develops punching speed, rhythm, endurance, accuracy, timing, reflexes, footwork, punching combinations, and counterpunching techniques.

By placing the mitts at various angles and levels, you can perform every conceivable kick, punch, or strike know to man. Properly utilized, focus mitts will refine your defensive reaction time and condition your entire body.

Focus mitts are constructed of durable leather designed to withstand tremendous punishment. Compared to other pieces of training equipment, the focus mitt is relatively inexpensive. However, an effective workout requires two mitts (one for each hand). You will also need a training partner (called the feeder) to hold the mitts. Your partner plays a vital role during your workouts by determining which combinations you will throw and their speed of delivery. In fact, the intensity of your workouts will depend largely upon his or her ability to manipulate the mitts and push you to your limit.

Heavy Bag Workout

To benefit from any focus-mitt workout, you must learn to concentrate intensely throughout the entire session. Block out all distractions. Try to visualize the mitt as a living, breathing opponent, not an inanimate target. This type of visualization will make all the difference in your training.

Here are few sample interval routines integrating the heavy bag with the focus mitts.

Beginner Level Interval Workout Routine (Focus Mitts)			
Round	Activity	Duration of Each Round	Rest Period
1	Heavy Bag	1 minute	2 minutes
2	Focus Mitts	2 minutes	1 minute
3	Heavy Bag	2 minutes	2 minutes
4	Focus Mitts	1 minute	1 minute
5	Heavy Bag	2 minutes	2 minutes
6	Focus Mitts	2 minutes	1 minute
7	Heavy Bag	1 minute	2 minutes
8	Focus Mitts	1 minute	1 minute

Intermediate Level
Interval Workout Routine (Focus Mitts)

Round	Activity	Duration of Each Round	Rest Period
1	Heavy Bag	2 minutes	2 minutes
2	Focus Mitts	2 minutes	1 minute
3	Heavy Bag	2 minutes	2 minutes
4	Focus Mitts	2 minutes	1 minute
5	Heavy Bag	2 minutes	2 minutes
6	Focus Mitts	2 minutes	1 minute
7	Heavy Bag	2 minutes	2 minutes
8	Focus Mitts	2 minutes	1 minute
9	Heavy Bag	2 minutes	2 minutes
10	Focus Mitts	2 minutes	2 minutes

I often tell my students that a good focus mitt feeder is one step ahead of his training partner, whereas a great focus mitt feeder is two steps ahead of his partner.

117

Advanced Level
Interval Workout Routine (Focus Mitts)

Round	Activity	Duration of Each Round	Rest Period
1	Heavy Bag	2 minutes	2 minutes
2	Focus Mitts	2 minutes	1 minute
3	Heavy Bag	3 minutes	2 minutes
4	Focus Mitts	3 minutes	1 minute
5	Heavy Bag	3 minutes	2 minutes
6	Focus Mitts	3 minutes	1 minute
7	Heavy Bag	3 minutes	2 minutes
8	Focus Mitts	3 minutes	1 minute
9	Heavy Bag	3 minutes	2 minutes
10	Focus Mitts	3 minutes	2 minutes
11	Heavy Bag	3 minutes	2 minutes
12	Focus Mitts	3 minutes	2 minutes

Unlike the heavy bag, the focus mitts are more forgiving on your wrists and hands and will allow you to progressively build up your power as your punching form improves.

Speed Bag Integration

The speed is used by boxers to develop coordination, endurance, timing, and rhythm. However, let me go on the record and state that I'm not a big fan of the speed bag. In fact, I believe it's an antiquated training tool that develops bad habits. Some include the following:

1. **Centerline exposure** - in order to strike the speed bag effectively, you must stand squarely in front of the bag. This means you must sacrifice your fighting stance and completely expose your centerline.

2. **Unrealistic attack rhythm** - the impact rhythm generated on a speed bag isn't remotely close to the attack rhythms used in real fighting.

3. **Improper fist positioning** - the speed bag requires you to *roll* your fists and strike it with the edge of your hands. If you would never punch this way in a real fight, then why on earth would you train this way?

4. **Poor body mechanics** - to maintain a fast striking rhythm on the bag, you must abandon proper punching mechanics.

5. **Mobility limitation** -since the speed bag is attached to a platform, your movement is significantly restricted. In fact, you must stay in close contact with the bag at all times.

6. **Lack of power** - to maintain the proper striking rhythm on the bag, you must only hit it with a slight amount of force. This style of punching is impractical for both the boxing ring and the street.

Nevertheless, I'm including the speed bag in this section out of respect for the boxing purist who insists on adding it to their training.

	Beginner Level		
	Interval Workout Routine (Speed Bag)		
Round	**Activity**	**Duration of Each Round**	**Rest Period**
1	Heavy Bag	1 minute	2 minutes
2	Speed Bag	2 minutes	1 minute
3	Heavy Bag	2 minutes	2 minutes
4	Speed Bag	1 minute	1 minute
5	Heavy Bag	2 minutes	2 minutes
6	Speed Bag	2 minutes	1 minute
7	Heavy Bag	1 minute	2 minutes
8	Speed Bag	1 minute	1 minute

When it comes to preparing for the ring or the street, remember to train the way you want to fight and fight the way you train!

Intermediate Level
Interval Workout Routine (Speed Bag)

Round	Activity	Duration of Each Round	Rest Period
1	Heavy Bag	2 minutes	2 minutes
2	Speed Bag	2 minutes	1 minute
3	Heavy Bag	2 minutes	2 minutes
4	Speed Bag	2 minutes	1 minute
5	Heavy Bag	2 minutes	2 minutes
6	Speed Bag	2 minutes	1 minute
7	Heavy Bag	2 minutes	2 minutes
8	Speed Bag	2 minutes	1 minute
9	Heavy Bag	2 minutes	2 minutes
10	Speed Bag	2 minutes	2 minutes

Remember to tighten your fists upon impact with bag. This action will allow your punches to travel with optimum speed and efficiency, and it will also augment the impact power of your strike.

Heavy Bag Workout

| \multicolumn{4}{c}{**Advanced Level**} |
| **Interval Workout Routine (Speed Bag)** | | | |
Round	Activity	Duration of Each Round	Rest Period
1	Heavy Bag	2 minutes	2 minutes
2	Speed Bag	2 minutes	1 minute
3	Heavy Bag	3 minutes	2 minutes
4	Speed Bag	3 minutes	1 minute
5	Heavy Bag	3 minutes	2 minutes
6	Speed Bag	3 minutes	1 minute
7	Heavy Bag	3 minutes	2 minutes
8	Speed Bag	3 minutes	1 minute
9	Heavy Bag	3 minutes	2 minutes
10	Speed Bag	3 minutes	2 minutes
11	Heavy Bag	3 minutes	2 minutes
12	Speed Bag	3 minutes	2 minutes

Workout Routine #12
Bare-Knuckle Training

While bag gloves are essential for protecting your hands when training, every once in a while you should workout without them. In fact, this type of bare-knuckle training is critical to anyone interested in reality-based self-defense training.

As I have stated in many of my other books, in the streets you don't have the luxury of rules, regulations or protective equipment. You have to make due with what you have at the moment of a high-risk self-defense encounter. Bare-knuckle training will help prepare you for the real thing. In fact, striking the heavy bag without hand protection is essential because it conditions your hands, knuckles, tendons, and joints for the rigors of street fighting.

However, bare-knuckle bag training is very hard on your wrists, hands, and knuckles. Transitioning from hand protected training to bare-knuckles is not easy. Initially, punching bare-fisted will feel awkward to even the most experienced fighter. Therefore, it's imperative to start out with approximately 25% of you punching power and increase it over a period of time.

Bare-knuckle training should only be performed on vinyl or soft leather bags. Do not use canvas heavy bags, they are made or coarse material that will lacerate your fingers and knuckles and permanently stain your heavy bag with blood.

One of the best ways to condition your hands and wrists for bare-knuckle fighting is to practice my *glove on/glove off* program. Essentially, you are going to alternate between bare handed and gloved punching. After several months, you can progress to exclusively bare-knuckle training.

What follows are several *glove on/glove off* workout routines.

Bare-knuckle fighting is a skill set that's much different from boxing and other combat sports. In fact, I know of several stories where professional boxers have broken their hands during a bare handed fist fight. This is because most professional fighters don't condition their hands for this type of fighting.

	Beginner Level		
Bare-Knuckle Training (Glove On/Glove Off)			
Round	Activity	Duration of Each Round	Rest Period
1	Glove on	1 minute	2 minutes
2	Glove off	30 seconds	1 minute
3	Glove on	2 minutes	2 minutes
4	Glove off	45 seconds	1 minute
5	Glove on	2 minutes	2 minutes
6	Glove off	1 minute	1 minute
7	Glove on	2 minutes	2 minutes
8	Glove off	90 seconds	1 minute

If bare-knuckle bag training is too hard on your hands, consider hitting the focus mitts instead. Unlike the heavy bag, the punching mitts are more forgiving on your knuckles.

Intermediate Level
Bare-Knuckle Training (Glove On/Glove Off)

Round	Activity	Duration of Each Round	Rest Period
1	Glove on	2 minutes	2 minutes
2	Glove off	1 minute	1 minute
3	Glove on	2 minutes	2 minutes
4	Glove off	90 seconds	1 minute
5	Glove on	2 minutes	2 minutes
6	Glove off	90 seconds	1 minute
7	Glove on	2 minutes	2 minutes
8	Glove off	2 minutes	1 minute
9	Glove on	2 minutes	2 minutes
10	Glove off	2 minutes	2 minutes

To avoid potential hand problems, don't perform bare-knuckle training more than three times per month.

Advanced Level
Bare-Knuckle Training (Glove On/Glove Off)

Round	Activity	Duration of Each Round	Rest Period
1	Glove on	2 minutes	2 minutes
2	Glove off	2 minutes	1 minute
3	Glove on	3 minutes	2 minutes
4	Glove off	2 minutes	1 minute
5	Glove on	3 minutes	2 minutes
6	Glove off	2 1/2 minutes	1 minute
7	Glove on	3 minutes	2 minutes
8	Glove off	2 1/2 minutes	1 minute
9	Glove on	3 minutes	2 minutes
10	Glove off	3 minutes	2 minutes
11	Glove on	3 minutes	2 minutes
12	Glove off	3 minutes	2 minutes

Proper breathing is one of the most important and often neglected aspects of bag work. Proper breathing promotes muscular relaxation and increases the speed and efficiency of your combinations. The rate at which you breathe will also determine how quickly your cardiorespiratory system can recover from a round.

127

Workout Routine #13
Pummel Training

Pummel training is designed for both mixed martial arts and street self-defense training. It requires you to attack the heavy bag from the top mounted position for specified period of time.

There are two punches that can be delivered from the mount position. They are:

- **Linear blast**
- **Short Arc Hammer Fist**

When performing both punches, remember to keep everything tight and aim for the center of the bag. Your objective is to punch through your target. When pummeling the heavy bag, you can vary the cadence of your punches from moderate to full speed.

Warning! Pummeling is a devastating self-defense technique that can severely injure your adversary and should only be used in life and death situations. Remember to always be certain that your actions are legally and morally justified in the eyes of the law.

To execute the pummel drill, apply the following steps:

1. Place a heavy bag on the floor.

2. Have your training partner tie a rope (approximately five feet long) to the top of the bag.

3. Mount the heavy bag (the same way you would mount an assailant in a ground fight).

4. Employ full-speed, full-force strikes on the upper portion of the heavy bag. Be vicious and attack the bag with all of the aggression you can muster.

5. Have your training partner pull vigorously (side to side, and up and down) on the rope while you deliver the blows. Strive to maintain a good base and avoid losing your balance when your partner tugs the bag.

6. Perform this drill for a minimum of five rounds.

The pummeling drill is conducted for a prolonged amount of time. This is done strictly for body mechanic mastery and muscular endurance. Never apply pummeling on a human being for a prolonged amount of time. Doing so can cause brain damage or death.

Pummeling Demonstration

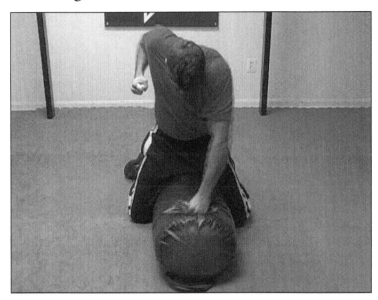

Step 1: The practitioner begins by throwing a left punch from the top mounted position.

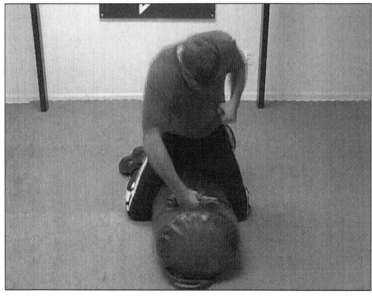

Step 2: He immediately follows with a right punch.

Step 3: He throws another left punch.

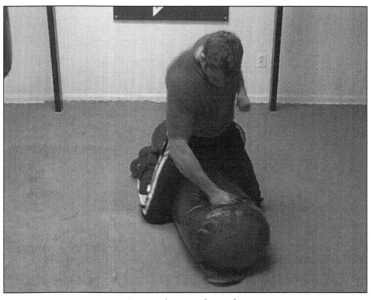

Step 4: Then another right.

Step 5: Followed by a left.

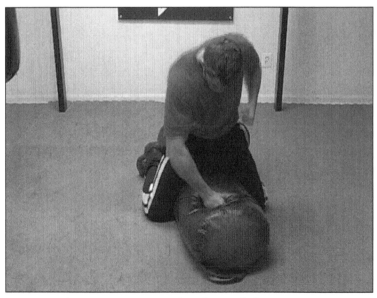

Step 6: He continues punching for a total of two minutes.

Beginner Level Pummel Drill		
Round	Duration of Each Round	Rest Period
1	30 seconds	2 minutes
2	45 seconds	2 minutes
3	45 seconds	2 minutes
4	1 minute	2 minutes
5	1 minute	2 minutes
6	1 minute	2 minutes
7	1 minute	2 minutes
8	1 minute	2 minutes

Heavy Bag Workout

Intermediate Level Pummel Drill		
Round	Duration of Each Round	Rest Period
1	1 minute	2 minutes
2	90 seconds	1 minute
3	2 minutes	2 minutes
4	2 minutes	1 minute
5	90 seconds	2 minutes
6	2 1/2 minutes	1 minute
7	2 minutes	2 minutes
8	1 minute	1 minute
9	3 minutes	2 minutes
10	3 minutes	2 minutes

Advanced Level Pummel Drill		
Round	Duration of Each Round	Rest Period
1	2 minutes	2 minutes
2	2 minutes	1 minute
3	3 minutes	2 minutes
4	2 minutes	1 minute
5	3 minutes	2 minutes
6	2 1/2 minutes	1 minute
7	3 minutes	2 minutes
8	2 1/2 minutes	1 minute
9	3 minutes	2 minutes
10	3 minutes	2 minutes
11	4 minutes	2 minutes
12	4 minutes	2 minutes

Workout Routine #14
Impairment Training

Impairment training teaches you how to fight when temporarily injured or impaired. There are several different types of impairment training routines you can perform on the heavy bag. Let's take a look at one of them.

Disorientation Drill

The Disorientation drill replicates the lightheaded sensation you will feel when you get hit by the opponent. This exercise is particularly useful because it teaches you to continue fighting when you are dizzy and lose your balance during a fight. To perform the exercise, employ the following steps:

1. Start with both your hands at your sides and your head looking down at the floor.

2. Next, close your eyes and begin spinning your body in a clockwise direction.

3. Continue spinning for approximately 10 seconds.

4. After 10 seconds, your training partner calls out "fight!"

5. Immediately stop spinning, open your eyes and attack the heavy bag with a barrage of punching combinations. Remember, you're going to be very dizzy, so do your best to maintain proper punching form.

6. Continue punching the heavy bag for approximately 20 seconds.

7. Rest for a minimum of 5 minutes before going again.

Disorientation Drill Demonstration

Step 1: The practitioner begins with his head down, eyes closed, and his arms at his sides.

Step 2: The time keeper instructs him to begin spinning.

Step 3: The man starts to spin his body in a clockwise direction.

Step 4: He continues to spin with his eyes closed for approximately 10 seconds.

Step 5: At the end of 10 seconds, the time keeper yells, "fight!"

139

Step 6: The practitioner immediately opens his eyes and tries to balance himself.

Step 7: He moves toward the bag.

Step 8: Despite his dizziness, he begins punching the heavy bag.

Step 9: After his second punch, the drill takes effect.

Step 10: The practitioner loses his balance.

Step 11: And falls to side.

Step 12: He crashes into the wall.

Step 13: He quickly regains his balance and goes after the bag once more.

Step 14: He resumes punching the heavy bag.

Step 15: He continues hitting the bag for approximately 20 seconds.

144

Step 16: The practitioner is clearly disoriented at the completion of the drill.

Be very careful when practicing the disorientation drill. Make certain your training area is away from windows, glass doors objects, children, and pets.

Disorientation Drill Workout Routines				
Skill Level	Duration of Spin	Duration of Punching Round	Rest Period Between Rounds	Total Number of rounds
Beginner	5 seconds	10 seconds	10 minutes	2
Beginner	5 seconds	12 seconds	10 minutes	2
Beginner	8 seconds	14 seconds	10 minutes	2
Beginner	8 seconds	15 seconds	10 minutes	2
Intermediate	10 seconds	15 seconds	5 minutes	3
Intermediate	10 seconds	20 seconds	5 minutes	3
Intermediate	10 seconds	20 seconds	5 minutes	3
Intermediate	10 seconds	25 seconds	5 minutes	3
Advanced	10 seconds	25 seconds	5 minutes	4
Advanced	10 seconds	30 seconds	5 minutes	4
Advanced	10 seconds	45 seconds	5 minutes	4
Advanced	10 seconds	45 seconds	5 minutes	4

Other Impairment Drills

There are many other impairment drills that you can perform. Here are a few suggestions that will get you started.

1. Workout on the heavy bag with one arm in a sling.

2. Wear an eye patch and see how it affects your punching skills.

3. Train when you are suffering from a hangover.

4. Wear a weight vest when training.

5. Wear an elevation training mask when working out on the heavy bag.

6. Want to experience some real physical discomfort, try working out on the bag with a marble in your shoe.

7. To replicate unstable terrain, workout with sand, gravel or sawdust on the floor (be careful).

8. Practice hitting the bag with a light source beaming into your face.

9. Workout under poor lighting conditions.

10. Be creative, you are only limited by your imagination.

Heavy Bag Workout

Heavy Bag Resources

Heavy Bag Videos

If you wish to explore additional information about heavy bag training, I encourage you to check out the following video and book resources. Instructional videos include the following:

- *Heavy Bag Training*
- *Punching Bag Combinations*

Both videos are available for purchase on my website and amazon.com

Heavy Bag Training DVD

Punching Bag Combinations DVD

Heavy Bag Books

You can also find the entire heavy bag training book series at amazon.com. They are available in both paperback and kindle editions.

Heavy Bag Training
Book #1

Heavy Bag Combinations
Book #2

Appendix

Foundational Heavy Bag Skills

In this section, I am going to teach you the foundational fighting techniques required to perform all of the heavy bag workout routines featured in this book. These basic skills include the fighting stance, footwork, jab, rear cross, hooks and uppercuts. Let's begin with the fighting stance..

The Fighting Stance

The fighting stance defines your ability to execute both offensive and defensive techniques, and it will play a material role in the outcome of a fight. It stresses strategic soundness and simplicity over complexity and style. The fighting stance also facilitates optimum execution of your body weapons while simultaneously protecting your vital targets against quick counter strikes.

The fighting stance is designed around the centerline. The centerline is an imaginary vertical line running through the center of the body, from the top of your head to the bottom of the groin. Most of your vital targets are situated along this line, including the head, throat, solar plexus, and groin. Obviously, you want to avoid directly exposing your centerline to the assailant. To achieve this, position your feet and body at a 45-degree angle

Pictured here, a left lead fighting stance.

152

from the opponent. This moves your body targets back and away from direct strikes but leaves you strategically positioned to attack.

When assuming a fighting stance, place your strongest and most coordinated side forward. For example, a right-handed person stands with his or her right side toward the assailant. Keeping your strongest side forward enhances the speed, power, and accuracy of your strike. This doesn't mean that you should never practice fighting from your other side. You must be capable of fighting from both sides, and you should spend equal practice time on the left and right stances.

Many people make the costly mistake of stepping forward to assume a fighting stance. Do not do this! This action only moves you closer to your assailant before your protective structure is soundly established. Moving closer to your assailant also dramatically reduces your defensive reaction time. So get into the habit of stepping backward to assume your stance. Practice this daily until it becomes a natural and economical movement.

How to Assume a Fighting Stance

When assuming your fighting stance, place your feet about shoulder width apart. Keep your knees bent and flexible. Think of your legs as power springs to launch you through the ranges of unarmed combat (kicking, punching, and grappling range).

Mobility is also important, as we'll discuss later. All footwork and strategic movement should be performed on the balls of your feet. Your weight distribution is also an important factor. Since combat is dynamic, your weight distribution will frequently change. However, when stationary, keep 50 percent of your body weight on each leg and always be in control of it.

The hands are aligned one behind the other along your centerline. The lead arm is held high and bent at approximately 90 degrees. The rear arm is kept back by the chin. Arranged this way, the hands not only protect the upper centerline but also allow quick deployment of your body weapons. When holding your guard, do not tighten your shoulder or arm muscles prior to striking. Stay relaxed and loose. Finally, keep your chin slightly angled down. This diminishes target size and reduces the likelihood of a paralyzing blow to your chin or a lethal strike to your throat.

The best method for practicing your fighting stance is in front of a full-length mirror. Place the mirror in an area that allows sufficient room for movement; a garage or basement is perfect. Stand in front of the mirror, far enough away to see your entire body. Stand naturally with your arms relaxed at your sides. Now close your eyes and quickly assume your fighting stance. Open your eyes and check for flaws. Look for low hand guards, improper foot positioning or body angle, rigid shoulders and knees, etc. Drill this way repeatedly, working from both the right and left side. Practice this until your fighting stance becomes second nature.

Footwork & Mobility

Next are footwork and mobility. I define mobility as the ability to move your body quickly and freely, which is accomplished through basic footwork. The safest footwork involves quick, economical steps performed on the balls of your feet, while you remain relaxed and balanced. Keep in mind that balance is your most important consideration.

Basic footwork can be used for both offensive and defensive purposes, and it is structured around four general directions: forward, backward, right, and left. However, always remember this footwork rule of thumb: Always move the foot closest to the direction you want to go first, and let the other foot follow an equal distance. This prevents cross-stepping, which can cost you your life in a high-risk combat situation.

Basic Footwork Movements

1. Moving forward (advance)- from your fighting stance, first move your front foot forward (approximately 12 inches) and then move your rear foot an equal distance.

2. Moving backward (retreat) - from your fighting stance, first move your rear foot backward (approximately 12 inches) and then move your front foot an equal distance.

3. Moving right (sidestep right) - from your fighting stance, first move your right foot to the right (approximately 12 inches) and then move your left foot an equal distance.

4. Moving left (sidestep left) - from your fighting stance, first move your left foot to the left (approximately 12 inches) and then move your right foot an equal distance.

Practice these four movements for 10 to 15 minutes a day in front of a full-length mirror. In a couple weeks, your footwork should be quick, balanced, and natural.

Circling Right and Left

Strategic circling is an advanced form of footwork where you will use your front leg as a pivot point. This type of movement can also be used defensively to evade an overwhelming assault or to strike the opponent from various strategic angles. Strategic circling can be performed from either a left or right stance.

Circling left (from a left stance) - this means you'll be moving your body around the opponent in a clockwise direction. From a left stance, step 8 to 12 inches to the left with your left foot, then use your left leg as a pivot point and wheel your entire rear leg to the left until the correct stance and positioning is acquired.

Circling right (from a right stance) - from a right stance, step 8 to 12 inches to the right with your right foot, then use your right leg as a pivot point and wheel your entire rear leg to the right until the correct stance and positioning is acquired.

Punching Techniques

In this section, I'm going to teach you four different punching skills that you will be using during you heavy bag workouts. They are:

- **Jab**
- **Rear cross (aka Straight Right)**
- **Hook punch**
- **Uppercut punch**

The Jab

The jab is a linear punch thrown from your lead arm, and contact is made with the center knuckle. To execute the technique, perform the following steps.

1. Start off in a fighting stance with both of your hands held up in the guard position. Your fists should be lightly clenched with both of your elbows pointing to the ground.

2. Simultaneously step toward the opponent and twist your front waist and shoulder forward as you snap your front arm into the target.

3. When delivering the punch, remember not to lock out your arm as this will have a "pushing effect" on the target.

4. Quickly retract your arm back to the starting position.

5. One common mistake when throwing the punch is to let it deflect off to the side of the target. Also, keep in mind that jabs can be delivered to the opponent's head or body. Targets for the punch include the opponent's nose, chin, and solar plexus.

Pictured here, the jab.

Rear Cross or Straight Right

The rear cross is considered the heavy artillery of punches and it's thrown from your rear arm. To execute the punch, perform the following steps:

1. Start off in a fighting stance with both of your hands held up in the guard position. Your fists should be lightly clenched with both of your elbows pointing to the ground.

2. Next, quickly twist your rear hips and shoulders forward as you snap your rear arm into the target. Proper waist twisting and weight transfer is of paramount importance to the rear cross. You must shift your weight from your rear foot to your lead leg as you throw the punch.

3. To maximize the impact of the punch, make certain that your fist is positioned horizontally. Avoid overextending the blow or exposing your chin during its execution.

157

4. Once again, do not lock out your arm when throwing the punch. Let the power of the blow sink into the target before you retract it back to the starting position.

Hook Punch

The hook is another devastating punch in your arsenal, yet it's also one of the most difficult to master. This punch can be performed

The rear cross.

from either your front or rear hand, and it can be delivered to both high or low targets.

1. Start in a fighting stance with your hand guard held up. Both of your elbows should be pointing to the ground, and your fists clenched loosely.

2. Next, quickly and smoothly, raise your elbow up so that your arm is parallel to the ground while simultaneously torquing your shoulder, hip, and foot into the direction of the blow.

3. When delivering the strike, be certain your arm is bent at

158

least ninety degrees and that your wrist and forearm are kept straight throughout the movement.

4. As you throw the punch, your fist is positioned vertically. The elbow should be locked when contact is made with the target. Remember to simultaneously tighten your fists when impact is made with the target. This action will allow your punch to travel with optimum speed and efficiency, and it will also augment the impact power of your strike.

5. Return to the starting position.

Uppercut Punch

The uppercut is a another powerful punch that can be delivered

The lead hook punch.

from both the lead and rear arm. To execute the blow, perform the following steps.

1. Start off in a fighting stance with both of your hands held up

in the guard position. Your fists should be lightly clenched with both of your elbows pointing to the ground.

2. Next, drop your shoulder and bend your knees.

3. Quickly, stand up and drive your fist upward and into the target. Your palm should be facing you when contact is made with the target. To avoid any possible injury, always keep your wrists straight.

4. Make certain your punch has a tight arc. Avoid "winding up" the blow. A properly executed uppercut punch should be a tight explosive jolt.

5. Return to the fighting stance.

The rear uppercut.

The lead uppercut punch.

Glossary

A

accuracy—The precise or exact projection of force. Accuracy is also defined as the ability to execute a combative movement with precision and exactness.

adaptability—The ability to physically and psychologically adjust to new or different conditions or circumstances of combat.

advanced first-strike tools—Offensive techniques that are specifically used when confronted with multiple opponents.

aerobic exercise—Literally, "with air." Exercise that elevates the heart rate to a training level for a prolonged period of time, usually 30 minutes.

affective preparedness – One of the three components of preparedness. Affective preparedness means being emotionally, philosophically, and spiritually prepared for the strains of combat. See cognitive preparedness and psychomotor preparedness.

aggression—Hostile and injurious behavior directed toward a person.

aggressive response—One of the three possible counters when assaulted by a grab, choke, or hold from a standing position. Aggressive response requires you to counter the enemy with destructive blows and strikes. See moderate response and passive response.

aggressive hand positioning—Placement of hands so as to imply aggressive or hostile intentions.

agility—An attribute of combat. One's ability to move his or her body quickly and gracefully.

amalgamation—A scientific process of uniting or merging.

ambidextrous—The ability to perform with equal facility on both the right and left sides of the body.

anabolic steroids – synthetic chemical compounds that resemble the male sex hormone testosterone. This performance-enhancing drug is known to increase lean muscle mass, strength, and endurance.

analysis and integration—One of the five elements of CFA's mental component. This is the painstaking process of breaking down various elements, concepts, sciences, and disciplines into their atomic parts, and then methodically and strategically analyzing, experimenting, and drastically modifying the information so that it fulfills three combative requirements: efficiency, effectiveness, and safety. Only then is it finally integrated into the CFA system.

anatomical striking targets—The various anatomical body targets that can be struck and which are especially vulnerable to potential harm. They include: the eyes, temple, nose, chin, back of neck, front of neck, solar plexus, ribs, groin, thighs, knees, shins, and instep.

anchoring – The strategic process of trapping the assailant's neck or limb in order to control the range of engagement during razing.

assailant—A person who threatens or attacks another person.

assault—The threat or willful attempt to inflict injury upon the person of another.

assault and battery—The unlawful touching of another person without justification.

assessment—The process of rapidly gathering, analyzing, and accurately evaluating information in terms of threat and danger. You can assess people, places, actions, and objects.

attack—Offensive action designed to physically control, injure, or kill another person.

attitude—One of the three factors that determine who wins a street fight. Attitude means being emotionally, philosophically, and spiritually liberated from societal and religious mores. See skills and knowledge.

attributes of combat—The physical, mental, and spiritual qualities that enhance combat skills and tactics.

awareness—Perception or knowledge of people, places, actions, and objects. (In CFA, there are three categories of tactical awareness: criminal awareness, situational awareness, and self-awareness.)

B

balance—One's ability to maintain equilibrium while stationary or moving.

blading the body—Strategically positioning your body at a 45-degree angle.

blitz and disengage—A style of sparring whereby a fighter moves into a range of combat, unleashes a strategic compound attack, and then quickly disengages to a safe distance. Of all sparring methodologies, the blitz and disengage most closely resembles a real street fight.

block—A defensive tool designed to intercept the assailant's attack by placing a non-vital target between the assailant's strike and your vital body target.

body composition—The ratio of fat to lean body tissue.

body language—Nonverbal communication through posture, gestures, and facial expressions.

body mechanics—Technically precise body movement during the execution of a body weapon, defensive technique, or other fighting maneuver.

body tackle – A tackle that occurs when your opponent haphazardly rushes forward and plows his body into yours.

body weapon—Also known as a tool, one of the various body parts that can be used to strike or otherwise injure or kill a criminal assailant.

burn out—A negative emotional state acquired by physically over- training. Some symptoms include: illness, boredom, anxiety, disinterest in training, and general sluggishness.

C

cadence—Coordinating tempo and rhythm to establish a timing pattern of movement.

cardiorespiratory conditioning—The component of physical fitness that deals with the heart, lungs, and circulatory system.

centerline—An imaginary vertical line that divides your body in half and which contains many of your vital anatomical targets.

choke holds—Holds that impair the flow of blood or oxygen to the brain.

circular movements—Movements that follow the direction of a curve.

close-quarter combat—One of the three ranges of knife and bludgeon combat. At this distance, you can strike, slash, or stab your assailant with a variety of close-quarter techniques.

cognitive development—One of the five elements of CFA's mental component. The process of developing and enhancing your fighting skills through specific mental exercises and techniques. See analysis and integration, killer instinct, philosophy, and strategic/tactical development.

cognitive exercises—Various mental exercises used to enhance fighting skills and tactics.

cognitive preparedness – One of the three components of preparedness. Cognitive preparedness means being equipped with the strategic concepts, principles, and general knowledge of combat. See affective preparedness and psychomotor preparedness.

combat-oriented training—Training that is specifically related to the harsh realities of both armed and unarmed combat. See ritual-oriented training and sport-oriented training.

combative arts—The various arts of war. See martial arts.

combative attributes—See attributes of combat.

combative fitness—A state characterized by cardiorespiratory and muscular/skeletal conditioning, as well as proper body composition.

combative mentality—Also known as the killer instinct, this is a combative state of mind necessary for fighting. See killer instinct.

combat ranges—The various ranges of unarmed combat.

combative utility—The quality of condition of being combatively useful.

combination(s)—See compound attack.

common peroneal nerve—A pressure point area located approximately four to six inches above the knee on the midline of the outside of the thigh.

composure—A combative attribute. Composure is a quiet and focused mind-set that enables you to acquire your combative agenda.

compound attack—One of the five conventional methods of attack. Two or more body weapons launched in strategic succession whereby the fighter overwhelms his assailant with a flurry of full speed, full-force blows.

conditioning training—A CFA training methodology requiring the practitioner to deliver a variety of offensive and defensive combinations for a 4-minute period. See proficiency training and street training.

contact evasion—Physically moving or manipulating your body to avoid being tackled by the adversary.

Contemporary Fighting Arts—A modern martial art and self-defense system made up of three parts: physical, mental, and spiritual.

conventional ground-fighting tools—Specific ground-fighting techniques designed to control, restrain, and temporarily incapacitate your adversary. Some conventional ground fighting tactics include: submission holds, locks, certain choking techniques, and specific striking techniques.

coordination—A physical attribute characterized by the ability to perform a technique or movement with efficiency, balance, and accuracy.

counterattack—Offensive action made to counter an assailant's initial attack.

courage—A combative attribute. The state of mind and spirit that enables a fighter to face danger and vicissitudes with confidence, resolution, and bravery.

creatine monohydrate—A tasteless and odorless white powder that mimics some of the effects of anabolic steroids. Creatine is a safe body-building product that can benefit anyone who wants to increase their strength, endurance, and lean muscle mass.

criminal awareness—One of the three categories of CFA awareness. It involves a general understanding and knowledge of the nature and dynamics of a criminal's motivations, mentalities, methods, and capabilities to perpetrate violent crime. See situational awareness and self-awareness.

criminal justice—The study of criminal law and the procedures associated with its enforcement.

criminology—The scientific study of crime and criminals.

cross-stepping—The process of crossing one foot in front of or behind the other when moving.

crushing tactics—Nuclear grappling-range techniques designed to crush the assailant's anatomical targets.

cue word - a unique word or personal statement that helps focus your attention on the execution of a skill, instead of its outcome.

D

deadly force—Weapons or techniques that may result in unconsciousness, permanent disfigurement, or death.

deception—A combative attribute. A stratagem whereby you delude your assailant.

decisiveness—A combative attribute. The ability to follow a tactical course of action that is unwavering and focused.

defense—The ability to strategically thwart an assailant's attack (armed or unarmed).

defensive flow—A progression of continuous defensive responses.

defensive mentality—A defensive mind-set.

defensive reaction time—The elapsed time between an assailant's physical attack and your defensive response to that attack. See offensive reaction time.

demeanor—A person's outward behavior. One of the essential factors to consider when assessing a threatening individual.

diet—A lifestyle of healthy eating.

disingenuous vocalization—The strategic and deceptive

utilization of words to successfully launch a preemptive strike at your adversary.

distancing—The ability to quickly understand spatial relationships and how they relate to combat.

distractionary tactics—Various verbal and physical tactics designed to distract your adversary.

double-end bag—A small leather ball hung from the ceiling and anchored to the floor with bungee cord. It helps develop striking accuracy, speed, timing, eye-hand coordination, footwork and overall defensive skills.

double-leg takedown—A takedown that occurs when your opponent shoots for both of your legs to force you to the ground.

E

ectomorph—One of the three somatotypes. A body type characterized by a high degree of slenderness, angularity, and fragility. See endomorph and mesomorph.

effectiveness—One of the three criteria for a CFA body weapon, technique, tactic, or maneuver. It means the ability to produce a desired effect. See efficiency and safety.

efficiency—One of the three criteria for a CFA body weapon, technique, tactic, or maneuver. It means the ability to reach an objective quickly and economically. See effectiveness and safety.

emotionless—A combative attribute. Being temporarily devoid of human feeling.

endomorph—One of the three somatotypes. A body type characterized by a high degree of roundness, softness, and body fat. See ectomorph and mesomorph.

evasion—A defensive maneuver that allows you to strategically maneuver your body away from the assailant's strike.

evasive sidestepping—Evasive footwork where the practitioner moves to either the right or left side.

evasiveness—A combative attribute. The ability to avoid threat or danger.

excessive force—An amount of force that exceeds the need for a particular event and is unjustified in the eyes of the law.

experimentation—The painstaking process of testing a combative hypothesis or theory.

explosiveness—A combative attribute that is characterized by a sudden outburst of violent energy.

F

fear—A strong and unpleasant emotion caused by the anticipation or awareness of threat or danger. There are three stages of fear in order of intensity: fright, panic, and terror. See fright, panic, and terror.

feeder—A skilled technician who manipulates the focus mitts.

femoral nerve—A pressure point area located approximately 6 inches above the knee on the inside of the thigh.

fighting stance—Any one of the stances used in CFA's system. A strategic posture you can assume when face-to-face with an unarmed assailant(s). The fighting stance is generally used after you have launched your first-strike tool.

fight-or-flight syndrome—A response of the sympathetic nervous system to a fearful and threatening situation, during which it prepares your body to either fight or flee from the perceived danger.

finesse—A combative attribute. The ability to skillfully execute a movement or a series of movements with grace and refinement.

first strike—Proactive force used to interrupt the initial stages of an assault before it becomes a self-defense situation.

first-strike principle—A CFA principle that states that when physical danger is imminent and you have no other tactical option but to fight back, you should strike first, strike fast, and strike with authority and keep the pressure on.

first-strike stance—One of the stances used in CFA's system. A strategic posture used prior to initiating a first strike.

first-strike tools—Specific offensive tools designed to initiate a preemptive strike against your adversary.

fisted blows – Hand blows delivered with a clenched fist.

five tactical options – The five strategic responses you can make in a self-defense situation, listed in order of increasing level of resistance: comply, escape, de-escalate, assert, and fight back.

flexibility—The muscles' ability to move through maximum natural ranges. See muscular/skeletal conditioning.

focus mitts—Durable leather hand mitts used to develop and sharpen offensive and defensive skills.

footwork—Quick, economical steps performed on the balls of the feet while you are relaxed, alert, and balanced. Footwork is structured around four general movements: forward, backward, right, and left.

fractal tool—Offensive or defensive tools that can be used in more than one combat range.

fright—The first stage of fear; quick and sudden fear. See panic and terror.

full Beat – One of the four beat classifications in the Widow Maker Program. The full beat strike has a complete initiation and retraction phase.

G

going postal - a slang term referring to a person who suddenly and unexpectedly attacks you with an explosive and frenzied flurry of blows. Also known as postal attack.

grappling range—One of the three ranges of unarmed combat. Grappling range is the closest distance of unarmed combat from which you can employ a wide variety of close-quarter tools and techniques. The grappling range of unarmed combat is also divided into two planes: vertical (standing) and horizontal (ground fighting). See kicking range and punching range.

grappling-range tools—The various body tools and techniques that are employed in the grappling range of unarmed combat, including head butts; biting, tearing, clawing, crushing, and gouging tactics; foot stomps, horizontal, vertical, and diagonal elbow strikes, vertical and diagonal knee strikes, chokes, strangles, joint locks, and holds. See punching range tools and kicking range tools.

ground fighting—Also known as the horizontal grappling plane, this is fighting that takes place on the ground.

guard—Also known as the hand guard, this refers to a fighter's hand positioning.

guard position—Also known as leg guard or scissors hold, this is a ground-fighting position in which a fighter is on his back holding his opponent between his legs.

H

half beat – One of the four beat classifications in the Widow Maker Program. The half beat strike is delivered through the retraction phase of the proceeding strike.

hand positioning—See guard.

hand wraps—Long strips of cotton that are wrapped around the hands and wrists for greater protection.

haymaker—A wild and telegraphed swing of the arms executed by an unskilled fighter.

head-hunter—A fighter who primarily attacks the head.

heavy bag—A large cylindrical bag used to develop kicking, punching, or striking power.

high-line kick—One of the two different classifications of a kick. A kick that is directed to targets above an assailant's waist level. See low-line kick.

hip fusing—A full-contact drill that teaches a fighter to "stand his ground" and overcome the fear of exchanging blows with a stronger opponent. This exercise is performed by connecting two fighters with a 3-foot chain, forcing them to fight in the punching range of unarmed combat.

histrionics—The field of theatrics or acting.

hook kick—A circular kick that can be delivered in both kicking and punching ranges.

hook punch—A circular punch that can be delivered in both the punching and grappling ranges.

I

impact power—Destructive force generated by mass and velocity.

impact training—A training exercise that develops pain tolerance.

incapacitate—To disable an assailant by rendering him unconscious or damaging his bones, joints, or organs.

initiative—Making the first offensive move in combat.

inside position—The area between the opponent's arms, where he has the greatest amount of control.

intent—One of the essential factors to consider when assessing a threatening individual. The assailant's purpose or motive. See demeanor, positioning, range, and weapon capability.

intuition—The innate ability to know or sense something without the use of rational thought.

J

jersey Pull – Strategically pulling the assailant's shirt or jacket over his head as he disengages from the clinch position.

joint lock—A grappling-range technique that immobilizes the assailant's joint.

K

kick—A sudden, forceful strike with the foot.

kicking range—One of the three ranges of unarmed combat. Kicking range is the furthest distance of unarmed combat wherein you use your legs to strike an assailant. See grappling range and punching range.

kicking-range tools—The various body weapons employed in the kicking range of unarmed combat, including side kicks, push kicks, hook kicks, and vertical kicks.

killer instinct—A cold, primal mentality that surges to your consciousness and turns you into a vicious fighter.

kinesics—The study of nonlinguistic body movement communications. (For example, eye movement, shrugs, or facial gestures.)

kinesiology—The study of principles and mechanics of human movement.

kinesthetic perception—The ability to accurately feel your body during the execution of a particular movement.

knowledge—One of the three factors that determine who will win a street fight. Knowledge means knowing and understanding how to fight. See skills and attitude.

L

lead side -The side of the body that faces an assailant.

leg guard—See guard position.

linear movement—Movements that follow the path of a straight line.

low-maintenance tool—Offensive and defensive tools that require the least amount of training and practice to maintain proficiency. Low maintenance tools generally do not require preliminary stretching.

low-line kick—One of the two different classifications of a kick. A kick that is directed to targets below the assailant's waist level. (See high-line kick.)

lock—See joint lock.

M

maneuver—To manipulate into a strategically desired position.

MAP—An acronym that stands for moderate, aggressive, passive. MAP provides the practitioner with three possible responses to various grabs, chokes, and holds that occur from a standing position. See aggressive response, moderate response, and passive response.

Marathon des Sables (MdS) - a six-day, 156-mile ultramarathon held in southern Morocco, in the Sahara Desert. It is considered by many to be the toughest footrace on earth.

martial arts—The "arts of war."

masking—The process of concealing your true feelings from your opponent by manipulating and managing your body language.

mechanics—(See body mechanics.)

mental toughness - a performance mechanism utilizing a collection of mental attributes that allow a person to cope, perform and prevail through the stress of extreme adversity.

mental component—One of the three vital components of the CFA system. The mental component includes the cerebral aspects of fighting including the killer instinct, strategic and tactical development, analysis and integration, philosophy, and cognitive development. See physical component and spiritual component.

mesomorph—One of the three somatotypes. A body type classified by a high degree of muscularity and strength. The mesomorph possesses the ideal physique for unarmed combat. See ectomorph and endomorph.

mobility—A combative attribute. The ability to move your body quickly and freely while balanced. See footwork.

moderate response—One of the three possible counters when assaulted by a grab, choke, or hold from a standing position. Moderate response requires you to counter your opponent with a control and restraint (submission hold). See aggressive response and passive response.

modern martial art—A pragmatic combat art that has evolved to meet the demands and characteristics of the present time.

mounted position—A dominant ground-fighting position where a fighter straddles his opponent.

muscular endurance—The muscles' ability to perform the same

motion or task repeatedly for a prolonged period of time.

muscular flexibility—The muscles' ability to move through maximum natural ranges.

muscular strength—The maximum force that can be exerted by a particular muscle or muscle group against resistance.

muscular/skeletal conditioning—An element of physical fitness that entails muscular strength, endurance, and flexibility.

N

naked choke—A throat choke executed from the chest to back position. This secure choke is executed with two hands and it can be performed while standing, kneeling, and ground fighting with the opponent.

neck crush – A powerful pain compliance technique used when the adversary buries his head in your chest to avoid being razed.

neutralize—See incapacitate.

neutral zone—The distance outside the kicking range at which neither the practitioner nor the assailant can touch the other.

nonaggressive physiology—Strategic body language used prior to initiating a first strike.

nontelegraphic movement—Body mechanics or movements that do not inform an assailant of your intentions.

nuclear ground-fighting tools—Specific grappling range tools designed to inflict immediate and irreversible damage. Nuclear tools and tactics include biting tactics, tearing tactics, crushing tactics, continuous choking tactics, gouging techniques, raking tactics, and all striking techniques.

O

offense—The armed and unarmed means and methods of attacking a criminal assailant.

offensive flow—Continuous offensive movements (kicks, blows, and strikes) with unbroken continuity that ultimately neutralize or terminate the opponent. See compound attack.

offensive reaction time—The elapsed time between target selection and target impaction.

one-mindedness—A state of deep concentration wherein you are free from all distractions (internal and external).

ostrich defense—One of the biggest mistakes one can make when defending against an opponent. This is when the practitioner looks away from that which he fears (punches, kicks, and strikes). His mentality is, "If I can't see it, it can't hurt me."

P

pain tolerance—Your ability to physically and psychologically withstand pain.

panic—The second stage of fear; overpowering fear. See fright and terror.

parry—A defensive technique: a quick, forceful slap that redirects an assailant's linear attack. There are two types of parries: horizontal and vertical.

passive response—One of the three possible counters when assaulted by a grab, choke, or hold from a standing position. Passive response requires you to nullify the assault without injuring your adversary. See aggressive response and moderate response.

patience—A combative attribute. The ability to endure and tolerate difficulty.

perception—Interpretation of vital information acquired from your senses when faced with a potentially threatening situation.

philosophical resolution—The act of analyzing and answering various questions concerning the use of violence in defense of yourself and others.

philosophy—One of the five aspects of CFA's mental component. A deep state of introspection whereby you methodically resolve critical questions concerning the use of force in defense of yourself or others.

physical attributes—The numerous physical qualities that enhance your combative skills and abilities.

physical component—One of the three vital components of the CFA system. The physical component includes the physical aspects of fighting, such as physical fitness, weapon/technique mastery, and combative attributes. See mental component and spiritual component.

physical conditioning—See combative fitness.

physical fitness—See combative fitness.

positional asphyxia—The arrangement, placement, or positioning of your opponent's body in such a way as to interrupt your breathing and cause unconsciousness or possibly death.

positioning—The spatial relationship of the assailant to the assailed person in terms of target exposure, escape, angle of attack, and various other strategic considerations.

postal attack - see going postal.

power—A physical attribute of armed and unarmed combat. The amount of force you can generate when striking an anatomical target.

power generators—Specific points on your body that generate impact power. There are three anatomical power generators: shoulders, hips, and feet.

precision—See accuracy.

preemptive strike—See first strike.

premise—An axiom, concept, rule, or any other valid reason to modify or go beyond that which has been established.

preparedness—A state of being ready for combat. There are three components of preparedness: affective preparedness, cognitive preparedness, and psychomotor preparedness.

probable reaction dynamics - The opponent's anticipated or predicted movements or actions during both armed and unarmed combat.

proficiency training—A CFA training methodology requiring the practitioner to execute a specific body weapon, technique, maneuver, or tactic over and over for a prescribed number of repetitions. See conditioning training and street training.

proxemics—The study of the nature and effect of man's personal space.

proximity—The ability to maintain a strategically safe distance from a threatening individual.

pseudospeciation—A combative attribute. The tendency to assign subhuman and inferior qualities to a threatening assailant.

psychological conditioning—The process of conditioning the mind for the horrors and rigors of real combat.

psychomotor preparedness—One of the three components of preparedness. Psychomotor preparedness means possessing all of the physical skills and attributes necessary to defeat a formidable adversary. See affective preparedness and cognitive preparedness.

punch—A quick, forceful strike of the fists.

punching range—One of the three ranges of unarmed combat. Punching range is the mid range of unarmed combat from which the fighter uses his hands to strike his assailant. See kicking range and grappling range.

punching-range tools—The various body weapons that are employed in the punching range of unarmed combat, including finger jabs, palm-heel strikes, rear cross, knife-hand strikes, horizontal and shovel hooks, uppercuts, and hammer-fist strikes. See grappling-range tools and kicking-range tools.

Q

qualities of combat—See attributes of combat.

quarter beat - One of the four beat classifications of the Widow Maker Program. Quarter beat strikes never break contact with the assailant's face. Quarter beat strikes are primarily responsible for creating the psychological panic and trauma when Razing.

R

range—The spatial relationship between a fighter and a threatening assailant.

range deficiency—The inability to effectively fight and defend in all ranges of combat (armed and unarmed).

range manipulation—A combative attribute. The strategic manipulation of combat ranges.

range proficiency—A combative attribute. The ability to effectively fight and defend in all ranges of combat (armed and unarmed).

ranges of engagement—See combat ranges.

ranges of unarmed combat—The three distances (kicking range, punching range, and grappling range) a fighter might physically engage with an assailant while involved in unarmed combat.

raze – To level, demolish or obliterate.

razer – One who performs the Razing methodology.

razing – The second phase of the Widow Maker Program. A series of vicious close quarter techniques designed to physically and psychologically extirpate a criminal attacker.

razing amplifier - a technique, tactic or procedure that magnifies the destructiveness of your razing technique.

reaction dynamics—see probable reaction dynamics.

reaction time—The elapsed time between a stimulus and the response to that particular stimulus. See offensive reaction time and defensive reaction time.

rear cross—A straight punch delivered from the rear hand that crosses from right to left (if in a left stance) or left to right (if in a right stance).

rear side—The side of the body furthest from the assailant. See lead side.

reasonable force—That degree of force which is not excessive for a particular event and which is appropriate in protecting yourself or others.

refinement—The strategic and methodical process of improving or perfecting.

relocation principle—Also known as relocating, this is a street-fighting tactic that requires you to immediately move to a new location (usually by flanking your adversary) after delivering a compound attack.

repetition—Performing a single movement, exercise, strike, or action continuously for a specific period.

research—A scientific investigation or inquiry.

rhythm—Movements characterized by the natural ebb and flow of related elements.

ritual-oriented training—Formalized training that is conducted without intrinsic purpose. See combat-oriented training and sport-oriented training.

S

safety—One of the three criteria for a CFA body weapon, technique, maneuver, or tactic. It means that the tool, technique, maneuver or tactic provides the least amount of danger and risk for the practitioner. See efficiency and effectiveness.

scissors hold—See guard position.

scorching – Quickly and inconspicuously applying oleoresin capsicum (hot pepper extract) on your fingertips and then razing your adversary.

self-awareness—One of the three categories of CFA awareness. Knowing and understanding yourself. This includes aspects of yourself which may provoke criminal violence and which will promote a proper and strong reaction to an attack. See criminal awareness and situational awareness.

self-confidence—Having trust and faith in yourself.

self-enlightenment—The state of knowing your capabilities, limitations, character traits, feelings, general attributes, and motivations. See self-awareness.

set—A term used to describe a grouping of repetitions.

shadow fighting—A CFA training exercise used to develop and refine your tools, techniques, and attributes of armed and unarmed combat.

sharking – A counter attack technique that is used when your adversary grabs your razing hand.

shielding wedge - a defensive maneuver used to counter an unarmed postal attack.

situational awareness—One of the three categories of CFA awareness. A state of being totally alert to your immediate surroundings, including people, places, objects, and actions. (See criminal awareness and self-awareness.)

skeletal alignment—The proper alignment or arrangement of your body. Skeletal alignment maximizes the structural integrity of striking tools.

skills—One of the three factors that determine who will win a street fight. Skills refers to psychomotor proficiency with the tools and techniques of combat. See Attitude and Knowledge.

slipping—A defensive maneuver that permits you to avoid an assailant's linear blow without stepping out of range. Slipping can be accomplished by quickly snapping the head and upper torso sideways (right or left) to avoid the blow.

snap back—A defensive maneuver that permits you to avoid an assailant's linear and circular blows without stepping out of range. The snap back can be accomplished by quickly snapping the head backward to avoid the assailant's blow.

somatotypes—A method of classifying human body types or builds into three different categories: endomorph, mesomorph, and ectomorph. See endomorph, mesomorph, and ectomorph.

sparring—A training exercise where two or more fighters fight each other while wearing protective equipment.

speed—A physical attribute of armed and unarmed combat. The rate or a measure of the rapid rate of motion.

spiritual component—One of the three vital components of the CFA system. The spiritual component includes the metaphysical issues and aspects of existence. See physical component and mental component.

sport-oriented training—Training that is geared for competition and governed by a set of rules. See combat-oriented training and ritual-oriented training.

sprawling—A grappling technique used to counter a double- or single-leg takedown.

square off—To be face-to-face with a hostile or threatening assailant who is about to attack you.

stance—One of the many strategic postures you assume prior to or during armed or unarmed combat.

stick fighting—Fighting that takes place with either one or two sticks.

strategic positioning—Tactically positioning yourself to either escape, move behind a barrier, or use a makeshift weapon.

strategic/tactical development—One of the five elements of CFA's mental component.

strategy—A carefully planned method of achieving your goal of engaging an assailant under advantageous conditions.

street fight—A spontaneous and violent confrontation between two or more individuals wherein no rules apply.

street fighter—An unorthodox combatant who has no formal training. His combative skills and tactics are usually developed in the street by the process of trial and error.

street training—A CFA training methodology requiring the practitioner to deliver explosive compound attacks for 10 to 20 seconds. See condition ng training and proficiency training.

strength training—The process of developing muscular strength through systematic application of progressive resistance.

stress - physiological and psychological arousal caused by a stressor.

stressors - any activity, situation, circumstance, event, experience, or condition that causes a person to experience both physiological and psychological stress.

striking art—A combat art that relies predominantly on striking techniques to neutralize or terminate a criminal attacker.

striking shield—A rectangular shield constructed of foam and vinyl used to develop power in your kicks, punches, and strikes.

striking tool—A natural body weapon that impacts with the assailant's anatomical target.

strong side—The strongest and most coordinated side of your body.

structure—A definite and organized pattern.

style—The distinct manner in which a fighter executes or performs his combat skills.

stylistic integration—The purposeful and scientific collection of tools and techniques from various disciplines, which are strategically integrated and dramatically altered to meet three essential criteria: efficiency, effectiveness, and combative safety.

submission holds—Also known as control and restraint techniques, many of these locks and holds create sufficient pain to cause the adversary to submit.

system—The unification of principles, philosophies, rules, strategies, methodologies, tools, and techniques of a particular method of combat.

T

tactic—The skill of using the available means to achieve an end.

target awareness—A combative attribute that encompasses five strategic principles: target orientation, target recognition, target selection, target impaction, and target exploitation.

target exploitation—A combative attribute. The strategic maximization of your assailant's reaction dynamics during a fight. Target exploitation can be applied in both armed and unarmed encounters.

target impaction—The successful striking of the appropriate anatomical target.

target orientation—A combative attribute. Having a workable knowledge of the assailant's anatomical targets.

target recognition—The ability to immediately recognize appropriate anatomical targets during an emergency self-defense situation.

target selection—The process of mentally selecting the appropriate anatomical target for your self-defense situation. This is predicated on certain factors, including proper force response, assailant's positioning, and range.

target stare—A form of telegraphing in which you stare at the anatomical target you intend to strike.

target zones—The three areas in which an assailant's anatomical targets are located. (See zone one, zone two and zone three.)

technique—A systematic procedure by which a task is accomplished.

telegraphic cognizance—A combative attribute. The ability to recognize both verbal and non-verbal signs of aggression or assault.

telegraphing—Unintentionally making your intentions known to your adversary.

tempo—The speed or rate at which you speak.

terminate—To kill.

terror—The third stage of fear; defined as overpowering fear. See fright and panic.

timing—A physical and mental attribute of armed and unarmed combat. Your ability to execute a movement at the optimum moment.

tone—The overall quality or character of your voice.

tool—See body weapon.

traditional martial arts—Any martial art that fails to evolve and change to meet the demands and characteristics of its present environment.

traditional style/system—See traditional martial arts.

training drills—The various exercises and drills aimed at perfecting combat skills, attributes, and tactics.

trap and tuck – A counter move technique used when the adversary attempts to raze you during your quarter beat assault.

U

unified mind—A mind free and clear of distractions and focused on the combative situation.

use of force response—A combative attribute. Selecting the appropriate level of force for a particular emergency self-defense situation.

V

viciousness—A combative attribute. The propensity to be extremely violent and destructive often characterized by intense savagery.

violence—The intentional utilization of physical force to coerce, injure, cripple, or kill.

visualization—Also known as mental visualization or mental imagery. The purposeful formation of mental images and scenarios in the mind's eye.

W

warm-up—A series of mild exercises, stretches, and movements designed to prepare you for more intense exercise.

weak side—The weaker and more uncoordinated side of your body.

weapon and technique mastery—A component of CFA's physical component. The kinesthetic and psychomotor development of a weapon or combative technique.

weapon capability—An assailant's ability to use and attack with a particular weapon.

webbing - The first phase of the Widow Maker Program. Webbing is a two hand strike delivered to the assailant's chin. It is called Webbing because your hands resemble a large web that wraps around the enemy's face.

widow maker – One who makes widows by destroying husbands.

widow maker program – A CFA combat program specifically designed to teach the law abiding citizen how to use extreme force when faced with immediate threat of unlawful deadly criminal attack. The Widow Maker program is divided into two phases or methodologies: Webbing and Razing.

Y

yell—A loud and aggressive scream or shout used for various strategic reasons.

Z

zero beat – One of the four beat classifications of the Widow Maker, Feral Fighting and Savage Street Fighting Programs. Zero beat strikes are full pressure techniques applied to a specific target until it completely ruptures. They include gouging, crushing, biting, and choking techniques.

zone one—Anatomical targets related to your senses, including the eyes, temple, nose, chin, and back of neck.

zone three—Anatomical targets related to your mobility, including thighs, knees, shins, and instep.

zone two—Anatomical targets related to your breathing, including front of neck, solar plexus, ribs, and groin.

About Sammy Franco

With over 30 years of experience, Sammy Franco is one of the world's foremost authorities on armed and unarmed self-defense. Highly regarded as a leading innovator in combat sciences, Mr. Franco was one of the premier pioneers in the field of "reality-based" self-defense and combat instruction.

Sammy Franco is perhaps best known as the founder and creator of Contemporary Fighting Arts (CFA), a state-of-the-art offensive-based combat system that is specifically designed for real-world self-defense. CFA is a sophisticated and practical system of self-defense, designed specifically to provide efficient and effective methods to avoid, defuse, confront, and neutralize both armed and unarmed attackers.

Sammy Franco has frequently been featured in martial art magazines, newspapers, and appeared on numerous radio and television programs. Mr. Franco has also authored numerous books, magazine articles, and editorials and has developed a popular library of instructional videos.

Sammy Franco's experience and credibility in the combat science is unequaled. One of his many accomplishments in this field includes the fact that he has earned the ranking of a Law Enforcement Master Instructor, and has designed, implemented, and taught officer survival training to the United States Border Patrol (USBP). He has instructed members of the US Secret Service, Military Special Forces,

193

Washington DC Police Department, Montgomery County, Maryland Deputy Sheriffs, and the US Library of Congress Police. Sammy Franco is also a member of the prestigious International Law Enforcement Educators and Trainers Association (ILEETA) as well as the American Society of Law Enforcement Trainers (ASLET) and he is listed in the "Who's Who Director of Law Enforcement Instructors."

Sammy Franco is also a nationally certified Law Enforcement Instructor in the following curricula: PR-24 Side-Handle Baton, Police Arrest and Control Procedures, Police Personal Weapons Tactics, Police Power Handcuffing Methods, Police Oleoresin Capsicum Aerosol Training (OCAT), Police Weapon Retention and Disarming Methods, Police Edged Weapon Countermeasures and "Use of Force" Assessment and Response Methods.

Mr. Franco regularly conducts dynamic and enlightening seminars on different aspects of combat training, mental toughness and achieving personal peak performance.

On a personal level, Sammy Franco is an animal lover, who will go to great lengths to assist and rescue animals. Throughout the years, he's rescued everything from turkey vultures to goats. However, his most treasured moments are always spent with his beloved German Shepherd dogs.

For more information about Mr. Franco, you can visit his website at **SammyFranco.com** or follow him on Twitter **@RealSammyFranco**

Other Books by Sammy Franco

HEAVY BAG TRAINING
For Boxing, Mixed Martial Arts and Self-Defense
(Heavy Bag Training Series Book 1)
by Sammy Franco

The heavy bag is one of the oldest and most recognizable pieces of training equipment. It's used by boxers, mixed martial artists, self-defense practitioners, and fitness enthusiasts. Unfortunately, most people don't know how to use the heavy bag correctly. Heavy Bag Training teaches you everything you ever wanted to know about working out on the heavy bag. In this one-of-a-kind book, world-renowned self-defense expert Sammy Franco provides you with the knowledge, skills, and attitude necessary to maximize the training benefits of the bag. 8.5 x 5.5, paperback, photos, illus, 172 pages.

HEAVY BAG COMBINATIONS
The Ultimate Guide to Heavy Bag Punching Combinations
(Heavy Bag Training Series Book 2)
by Sammy Franco

Heavy Bag Combinations is the second book in Sammy Franco's best-selling Heavy Bag Training Series. This unique book is your ultimate guide to mastering devastating heavy bag punching combinations. With over 300+ photographs and detailed step-by-step instructions, Heavy Bag Combinations provides beginner, intermediate and advanced heavy bag workout combinations that will challenge you for the rest of your life! In fact, even the most experienced athlete will advance his fighting skills to the next level and beyond. 8.5 x 5.5, paperback, photos, illus, 248 pages.

THE COMPLETE BODY OPPONENT BAG BOOK
by Sammy Franco

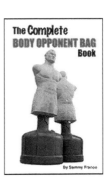

In this one-of-a-kind book, Sammy Franco teaches you the many hidden training features of the body opponent bag that will improve your fighting skills and boost your conditioning. With detailed photographs, step-by-step instructions, and dozens of unique workout routines, The Complete Body Opponent Bag Book is the authoritative resource for mastering this lifelike punching bag. It covers stances, punching, kicking, grappling techniques, mobility and footwork, targets, fighting ranges, training gear, time based workouts, punching and kicking combinations, weapons training, grappling drills, ground fighting, and dozens of workouts. 8.5 x 5.5, paperback, 139 photos, illustrations, 206 pages.

INVINCIBLE
Mental Toughness Techniques for
Peak Performance
by Sammy Franco

Invincible is a treasure trove of battle-tested techniques and strategies for improving mental toughness in all aspects of life. It teaches you how to unlock the true power of your mind and achieve success in sports, fitness, high-risk professions, self-defense, and other peak performance activities. However, you don't have to be an athlete or warrior to benefit from this unique mental toughness book. In fact, the mental skills featured in this indispensable program can be used by anyone who wants to reach their full potential in life. 8.5 x 5.5, paperback, photos, illus, 250 pages.

THE WIDOW MAKER PROGRAM
Extreme Self-Defense for Deadly Force Situations
by Sammy Franco

The Widow Maker Program is a shocking and revolutionary fighting style designed to unleash extreme force when faced with the immediate threat of an unlawful deadly criminal attack. In this unique book, self-defense innovator Sammy Franco teaches you his brutal and unorthodox combat style that is virtually indefensible and utterly devastating. With over 250 photographs and detailed step-by-step instructions, The Widow Maker Program teaches you Franco's surreptitious Webbing and Razing techniques. When combined, these two fighting methods create an unstoppable force capable of destroying the toughest adversary. 8.5 x 5.5, paperback, photos, illus, 218 pages.

FERAL FIGHTING
Advanced Widow Maker Fighting Techniques
by Sammy Franco

In this sequel, Sammy Franco marches forward with cutting-edge concepts and techniques that will take your self-defense skills to entirely new levels of combat performance. Feral Fighting includes Franco's revolutionary Shielding Wedge technique. When used correctly, it transforms you into an unstoppable human meat grinder, capable of destroying any criminal adversary. Feral Fighting also teaches you the cunning art or Scorching. Learn how to convert your fingertips into burning torches that generate over 2 million scoville heat units causing excruciating pain and temporarily blindness. 8.5 x 5.5, paperback, photos, illustrations, 204 pages.

196

MAXIMUM DAMAGE
Hidden Secrets Behind Brutal Fighting Combination
by Sammy Franco

Maximum Damage teaches you the quickest ways to beat your opponent in the street by exploiting his physical and psychological reactions in a fight. Learn how to stay two steps ahead of your adversary by knowing exactly how he will react to your strikes before they are delivered. In this unique book, reality based self-defense expert Sammy Franco reveals his unique Probable Reaction Dynamic (PRD) fighting method. Probable reaction dynamics are both a scientific and comprehensive offensive strategy based on the positional theory of combat. Regardless of your style of fighting, PRD training will help you overpower your opponent by seamlessly integrating your strikes into brutal fighting combinations that are fast, ferocious and final! 8.5 x 5.5, paperback, 240 photos, illustrations, 238 pages.

SAVAGE STREET FIGHTING
Tactical Savagery as a Last Resort
by Sammy Franco

In this revolutionary book, Sammy Franco reveals the science behind his most primal street fighting method. Savage Street Fighting is a brutal self-defense system specifically designed to teach the law-abiding citizen how to use "Tactical Savagery" when faced with the immediate threat of an unlawful deadly criminal attack. Savage Street Fighting is systematically engineered to protect you when there are no other self-defense options left! With over 300 photographs and detailed step-by-step instructions, Savage Street Fighting is a must-have book for anyone concerned about real world self-defense. Now is the time to learn how to unleash your inner beast! 8.5 x 5.5, paperback, 317 photos, illustrations, 232 pages.

FIRST STRIKE
End a Fight in Ten Seconds or Less!
by Sammy Franco

Learn how to stop any attack before it starts by mastering the art of the preemptive strike. First Strike gives you an easy-to-learn yet highly effective self-defense game plan for handling violent close-quarter combat encounters. First Strike will teach you instinctive, practical and realistic self-defense techniques that will drop any criminal attacker to the floor with one punishing blow. By reading this book and by practicing, you will learn the hard-hitting skills necessary to execute a punishing first strike and ultimately prevail in a self-defense situation. 8.5 x 5.5, paperback, photos, illustrations, 202 pages.

WAR MACHINE
How to Transform Yourself Into A Vicious & Deadly Street Fighter
by Sammy Franco

War Machine is a book that will change you for the rest of your life! When followed accordingly, War Machine will forge your mind, body and spirit into iron. Once armed with the mental and physical attributes of the War Machine, you will become a strong and confident warrior that can handle just about anything that life may throw your way. In essence, War Machine is a way of life. Powerful, intense, and hard. 11 x 8.5, paperback, photos, illustrations, 210 pages.

\KUBOTAN POWER
Quick and Simple Steps to Mastering the Kubotan Keychain
by Sammy Franco

With over 290 photographs and step-by-step instructions, Kubotan Power is the authoritative resource for mastering this devastating self-defense weapon. In this one-of-a-kind book, world-renowned self-defense expert, Sammy Franco takes thirty years of real-world teaching experience and gives you quick, easy and practical kubotan techniques that can be used by civilians, law enforcement personnel, or military professionals. The Kubotan is an incredible self-defense weapon that has helped thousands of people effectively defend themselves. Men, women, law enforcement officers, military, and security professionals alike, appreciate this small and discreet self-defense tool. Unfortunately, however, very little has been written about the kubotan, leaving it shrouded in both mystery and ignorance. As a result, most people don't know how to unleash the full power of this unique personal defense weapon. 8.5 x 5.5, paperback, 290 photos, illustrations, 204 pages.

CONTEMPORARY FIGHTING ARTS, LLC
"Real World Self-Defense Since 1989"
www.SammyFranco.com

198

20878947R00115

Printed in Great Britain
by Amazon